MW00701000

A SAVE–OUR–PLANET BOOK
THE PROFITS GO TO CONSERVATION

THE BIOTOPE AQUARIUM

An authentic imitation of nature in your home

Rainer Stawikowski

A school of Rosy Tetras in a community aquarium. Photo by Burkhard Kahl.

SETTING UP NATURAL-LOOKING AQUARIUMS

Contents

Originally published in German by Franckh-Kosmos Verlags-GmbH, Stuttgart, under the title *Fische im Biotop-Aquarium*. First edition © 1990 by Franckh-Kosmos Verlags-GmbH.

© Copyright 1993 by T.F.H. Publications, Inc. for English translation. A considerable amount of additional new material has been added to the literal German-English translation, including but not limited to additional photographs. Copyright is also claimed for this new material.

Distributed in the UNITED STATES to the Pet Trade by T.F.H. Publications, Inc., One T.F.H. Plaza, Neptune City, NJ 07753; distributed in the UNITED STATES to the Bookstore and Library Trade by National Book Network, Inc. 4720 Boston Way, Lanham MD 20706; in CANADA to the Pet Trade by H & L Pet Supplies Inc., 27 Kingston Crescent, Kitchener, Ontario N2B 2T6; Rolf C. Hagen Ltd., 3225 Sartelon Street, Montreal 382 Quebec; in CANADA to the Book Trade by Macmillan of Canada (A Division of Canada Publishing Corporation), 164 Commander Boulevard, Agincourt, Ontario M1S 3C7; in ENGLAND by T.F.H. Publications, PO Box 15, Waterlooville PO7 6BQ; in AUSTRALIA AND THE SOUTH PACIFIC by T.F.H. (Australia), Pty. Ltd., Box 149, Brookvale 2100 N.S.W., Australia; in NEW ZEALAND by Brooklands Aquarium Ltd., 5 McGiven Drive, New Plymouth, RD1 New Zealand; in the PHILIPPINES by Bio-Research, 5 Lippay Street, San Lorenzo Village, Makati, Rizal; in SOUTH AFRICA by Multipet Pty. Ltd., P.O. Box 35347, Northway, 4065, South Africa. Published by T.F.H. Publications, Inc. Manufactured in the United States of America by T.F.H. Publications, Inc.

What's a Biotope Aquarium

Freshwater aquaristics has changed in many respects over the years. At first our hobby dealt mainly with locally native species, but now tropical and subtropical species predominate.

There are many reasons for that change. One reason is that many native animal and plant species are now protected. Many species are endangered because their biotopes have been thoughtlessly destroyed. Now, the capture, keeping and breeding of endangered species are illegal. These species, however, are most certainly not being threatened, endangered or annihilated by aquarists or terrarium keepers! It's the pollution and annihilation of their native habitats that is to blame.

Another reason is that it's easier to heat than to cool an aquarium. There are, indeed, cooling devices, but they're not technically perfected, or else are too complex and expensive for the hobbyist. Yet many warmth-loving species can be kept quite satisfactorily in unheated aquariums at room

One of the collecting areas of the Rio Abacaxis in Brazil. Photo by H.-J. Richter.

temperature.

A third reason behind the preference for tropical and subtropical species today is the continued opening up of tropical regions on all continents where there are tropics, which has

At high water collecting fishes in this tangle of dead wood is virtually impossible. Photo by H.-J. Richter.

made a multitude of interesting species available to us.

Today's international air commerce has made it possible to import species from the far corners of the world, making the choice much greater than it was only

ten to twenty years ago. The possibility of illustrating many of these species in full color in books and periodicals, thus introducing them to many aquarists everywhere, has definitely contributed to their popularity. In addition, many of these species are quite suitable for keeping and

breeding.

There has also been an increase in the number of hobbyists who themselves travel to observe and collect fish and other animals in their native habitats. Such trips or expeditions provide not only plants and animals, but also a wealth of ecological information about many species. Much of this first-hand observation can be directly or indirectly applied to the keeping of plants and fish in aquariums.

Whoever has had the opportunity to visit fish biotopes in Africa, Asia, South America or Central America soon realizes that there are a plentitude of completely different habitats inhabited by various kinds of fish.

Altitude, subsoil characteristics, vegetation, and climate can all give a single body of water, say a river, innumerably different aspects as it goes from its source to its mouth. In the mountains, a river can be rocky, clear, rapid or even torrential, well oxygenated and cool,

Facing page. Aerial view of a river flowing into Lake Victoria. Notice how silty it is. Photo by Dr. H. R. Axelrod.

then become murky, very warm, sluggish and oxygen-deficient by the time it flows through the lowlands just before it reaches its mouth.

Ruggedly steep rocky banks alternate with densely overgrown banks, followed by stretches covered by large accumulations of dead wood. Finally there are sandy beaches and swampy zones.

Each of these habitats is characterized by its own fish fauna, including, of course, species that can also adapt to a variety of other, very different biotopes. Many species, however, are quite specialized to one habitat, which is more or less limited not only

spatially but also in other ways.

Some of these habitats or niches have absolutely nothing in common with the arrangement of an aquarium. It would be crazy to represent a biotope of muddy, turbid puddles in an aquarium and try to keep fish in it; no aquarist would attempt that.

On the other hand, there are biotopes which, because of their specific characteristics (clear water, vegetation, stones, woody roots, etc.), do challenge aquarists to regard them as models for an aquarium set-up.

This book will help you to reconstruct quite feasibly attainable biotopes in the aquarium. One thing

At low water in the Rio Abacaxis the many hiding places used by Discus and other fishes are exposed. The fishes will return to these areas as the water rises. Photo by H.-J. Richter.

Facing page: Top: Biotope of *Hemichromis* species in West Africa. Bottom Left: Biotope of *Pelvicachromis* species in West Africa. Bottom Right: Typical boulder-strewn shore of Lake Tanganyika. Photos by H.-J. Richter.

must be clear, however, and that is that any slavishly detailed and completely accurate representation is often impossible to achieve.

Such perfection, luckily, is not at all necessary, for most of our aquarium fish–despite their adaptation to specific niches–are quite tolerant within certain limits. For example, Malawi or Tanganyika cichlids, whose homes are characterized by rubble-covered or rocky shores, are not in the least disturbed in an aquarium with aquatic plants as long as they also have their stony decor. Their main concern is to have the stones available upon which to spawn and among which to hide themselves. Plants can be added as we see fit to please our own tastes.

We aren't using the concept of a "biotope aquarium" in any narrow sense, but quite broadly, allowing for compromises that can and often must be made.

All of my recommendations for biotope set-ups are mainly based upon assuring that each species has its vital needs (water movement and current for fish from river rapids, stones for fish from rocky shores, sandy bottom for fish

Young *Tropheus duboisi* find safety among the rubble strewn bottom of Lake Tanganyika. Photo by P. Brichard.

This is a typical biotope where *Ctenopoma maculatum* and *C. nanum* are found in southern Cameroon. Photo by H.-J. Richter.

from sandy areas, etc.). Then we try to reconstruct the most natural-looking habitat possible in an aquarium.

Aquarists and breeders always try to give their wards the best conditions to encourage them to reproduce easily. This requires the aquarist to constantly be on the lookout for ways to keep the fish healthy and happy in their home away from home. In other words, the natural biotope is reconstructed at least partially as it is in the wild. A biotope aquarium is not at all a new idea. The fact that so many fish successfully breed in aquariums shows that the concept of a biotope in a tank, at least within certain limits, is possible.

The fish discussed in this book are generally available in pet shops. Another possible way to obtain specific species is to contact the numerous associations and groups that specialize in the aquaristics and breeding of particular groups of fish (cichlids, labyrinthines, killifish, livebearing toothed carps, catfishes, stone loaches, etc.). Most of these organizations advertise in *Tropical Fish Hobbyist* magazine.

A few preliminary remarks about aquaristics.

Aquaristics has not only experienced a continuous flow of novel items, but also many valuable improvements in the tank itself. Today's

Typical set-up for an open spawner. This *Papiliochromis ramirezi* will probably spawn on the flat rock provided. Photo by H.-J. Richter.

usual sealant and adhesive techniques with silicon rubber have simplified tank construction and made much larger tanks possible than in the years when we had to be satisfied with either all-glass (blown-glass) tanks or with metal-framed ones into which the panes were cemented with window putty. Many tank manufacturers today produce tanks that measure over six feet in length, and these are in no way special orders, but standard stock items!

Heating and lighting, too, have changed. Even though the glass-rod heaters with built-in thermostat now available in pet shops still don't satisfy industrial standards, the heating of our tanks is now generally safer, simpler and more reliable. We can even choose among various types of aquarium heaters. There are heating pads and heating cables that go under the bottom of the tank so they don't come into contact with the water in the tank. Also, there are centrifugal or rotary pumps/outside filters (top or cup filters) provided with a heating device that not only decontaminates but also warms the water.

All of these systems are provided with reliable thermostats that assure constant water temperature once it's set.

Aquarium lighting, too, is now available in the

A community aquarium set-up that will safely house some of the larger dwarf cichlids along with various tetras. Photo by H.-J. Richter.

A community aquarium set up with plastic plants and a background simulating a rock wall. This combination of fishes is not the most compatible.

widest variety ever, too much to describe here. *Tropical Fish Hobbyist* contains sources on mercury, quartz, and other lighting systems.

Filtration, too, comes in a multitude of the most varied types and models. For small to moderately large tanks, air-driven inside filters generally suffice; these, like air pumps, come in many models and styles—nylon wadding or plastic inside filters filled with activated charcoal, sponge or foam material; there are also large-volume plastic housings filled with a pad of synthetic fiber, which, however, have the disadvantage of requiring a lot of space.

It's not really practical here to give general suggestions for choosing a filtration system. If you select an air-driven model, then don't make the mistake of trying to save money when buying your pump. Small ones (that are hardly efficient

A community aquarium set up with plastic plants and a background simulating a rock wall. This combination of fishes is not the most compatible.

Live plants and driftwood create a much more natural setting for a community aquarium. A better selection of fishes is also seen. Photo by B. Kahl.

and cheap in price and quality!) shut down very soon when in constant use and their filters are always in continuous operation.

Pet shops stock a great selection of outside filters in many styles, sizes and prices.

Compared with the inside filtration system, the outside system doesn't require your splashing around down in the water itself.

The disadvantage of the outside system is that you've got to play around with all the tubing and its connections, especially if they're plastic, which contains plasticizers or softeners; these substances eventually escape into the water,

where their effect on fish and plants is not yet known.

Also, this tubing eventually hardens and turns brittle, making the tubes difficult to handle. Rotary or centrifugal pumps are also available for inside filters. These pumps are generally attached on the edge of the tank above the surface of the water. A vertical tube leads down to the filter itself. Such rotary pumps associated with immersible extensions efficiently handle sizeable quantities of water hourly at surface level, but they can't lift the water.

For some time now, however, immersion rotary pumps have been available, whose motors are in watertight housings, so that the whole system can be placed underwater. These immersible pumps offer advantages: accidents caused by working pumps falling into the water are avoided; also, submerged pumps can generate water currents in the deeper parts of the tanks, which can produce remarkable effects in many species.

Today, many aquarists swear by so-called biological filters. These are basically still filtration vessels (boxes, vertical tubes, etc.) with filter material that offers the greatest possible surface area (clay tubes, clay potsherds, lava chunks, plastic "biogel,"

etc.). This surface is colonized by bacteria that break down toxic substances that get into the water.

There are wet- and dry-bed biological filters (percolating filters), whereby the water is led first in a closed circuit over the filter medium, then is transported out of the tank and over the filtration substrate. It drips over the substrate outside of the closed circuit before it once again finally enters the circulation.

Then there are aquarists who build (or have built) multichamber filters as either outside or inside filters. As inside filter, chambers of glass panes can be glued directly into the tank, and a multichamber

An aquarium set-up designed for open and cave spawners. Caves can also be created by rock formations. Photo by H.-J. Richter.

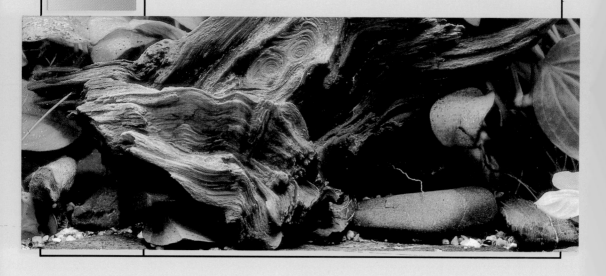

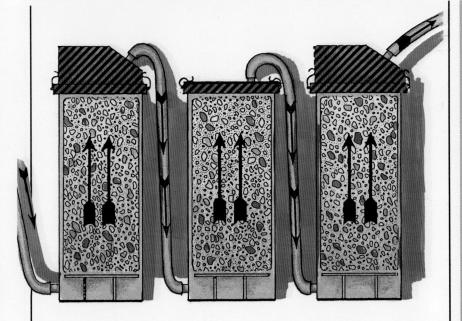

Diagram of three canister filters arranged in tandem for greater filtration power. Arrows show direction of water flow. Illustration by J. R. Quinn.

system set up as outside filter next to or behind the tank.

Fill each chamber with different filter substances so that you can use coarse substance as the pre-filter, and, in a chamber filled with finely divided substrate, remove finely divided contaminants from the water.

You can also add sedimentation chambers, where very coarse and heavy suspended matter can be deposited on the bottom.

Filters like that–driven by an appropriate rotary pump–are not only very efficient, but have a long operational life, since a regular cleaning of the coarse pre-filter substrate (large meshed nylon fiber fabric such as used for cup skimmers or cleaners, filter wadding, etc.) doesn't require much, all of which means that the finer substances in the rear chambers don't get contaminated too fast and clog.

The best sizes of tanks for the biotope set-ups discussed in the various chapters of this book as well as guidelines on techniques appear in the pertinent chapters.

Typical cold, rocky bottomed, high altitude, northern latitude stream. Photo by S. Kochetov

Clear-Water Rivers of the Central American Landbridge

The natural biotope and its residents

The Central American (or Meso-American) landbridge is one of the major volcanic regions of the world. Numerous volcanoes (of which most are now extinct), characterize the mountainous landscape of Mexico, Belize, Guatemala, El Salvador, Honduras, Nicaragua, Costa Rica and Panama.

In these mountains originate the many rivers that flow into the Pacific lowlands, to the Pacific Ocean or to the Atlantic slope, into the Gulf of Mexico and the Caribbean.

In large parts of Central America, the mountainous chains, which run more or less lengthwise along the landbridge, form an insurmountable watershed or divide for fish, so that we have both an Atlantic and a Pacific fish fauna.

Compared with other regions of the New

The Rio Unini, a tributary of the blackwater Rio Negro. The current could become quite swift here at times. Photo by Dr. H. R. Axelrod.

Many lakes are crystal clear at some times of the year but become much less so at other times, such as when there are plankton blooms. Photo by S. Kochetov.

World, such as the Amazon basin in South America, the rivers of Central America only have a short run from their source to their mouth. One of the largest river systems in Central America, the Rio Usumacinta, flows as a border between Mexico and Guatemala, and has a length of about 600 miles. That's about like the Rio Teles Pires in Brazil, which is only a tributary of the Rio Tapajos, which itself is "only" a feeder that runs into the mighty Amazon.

With such relatively short courses, in addition to the considerable differences in altitude the Central American rivers have to negotiate, the velocity of the water has to be rather high.

Then when heavy precipitation in the form of torrential downpours comes during the Central American rainy season, which lasts for several months, the rivers are transformed into raging torrents. As a result, rocks are torn from the mountains and washed down into the lowlands, where they accumulate in the river beds. That's why large quantities of rocky deposits characterize both the upper and lower courses of most rivers in this region.

The rocky appearance of the banks and subsoil of Central American rivers is characterized by round, polished gravel as large as a fist or even a soccer ball, or else by rough, weathered lava chunks, depending upon the nature of the terrain and the mountains. Only rarely does the traveler come upon areas where aquatic plants, say water lilies, give the biotope a completely different look.

The Central American river fish inhabit a place which is often a genuine

Many Central American rivers have clear water flowing rapidly over rocks and stones. This is Rio de la Sierra, which feeds the Rio Grijalva in southern Mexico. Photo by R. Stawikowski.

Typical Discus habitat of the Rio Abacaxis. Photo by Dr. H. R. Axelrod.

desert of rocks, at best broken here or there by an uprooted tree, its roots lifelessly high-ended up on shore.

It's mostly the cichlids that have successfully colonized this portion of the New World. Many of the approximately one hundred species that live here have adapted in a multitude of ways to their rocky surroundings.

The rocks provide food in the form of algae that colonize the rocks and stones in the sun-drenched relatively shallow water. This algae is the main food for many species that scrape it off with their rasp-like teeth.

Rocks are borders for the cichlids, which are territorial at least during spawning. Rocks are also hiding places, especially for the small and young fish that seek refuge in the nooks and crannies from their predators.

Rocks, too, are spawning grounds–really a highly polished substrate to which the open-brooding fish attach their large clutches of eggs. The mouth-brooding fish use the stony piles, crevices and fissures in the weathered rocks to protect their clutches of eggs from egg predators.

The mountains and rocky terrain have still another effect on the habitat of Central American freshwater fish. In many areas of this landbridge, the subsoil consists of calcareous minerals, such as for example, in northern Mexico, or consists of limestone karst, such as in the Mexican Yucatan Peninsula; this gives the river water a hardness that can reach 30°, 40°, 50° or even 60° dH.

The subsoil conditions also affect the acidity of the river water. The pH values are only rarely in the acid range, that is, less than 7, but are most often neutral or slightly alkaline (pH 7 to 8). That means that the fish here are not soft-water ones, such as, for example, most of the South American species, but are fish that prefer somewhat harder and more alkaline conditions, though many of them are quite adaptable and easy to care for.

As for the temperatures in the

Part of a 2-meter tank set up especially for Central American cichlids. Of importance are the stones and driftwood. The fish is the Black-banded Cichlid ("*Cichlasoma*" *maculicauda*). Photo by R. Stawikowski.

Other popular fishes that inhabit the Central American region are the poeciliids. This example is an aquarium strain of a swordtail, *Xiphophorus helleri*. Photo by Dr. H. Grier.

rivers of Central America, they are generally lower in the waters at higher altitudes, that is, at the rivers' sources, than in the lowland rivers towards their mouths.

During the rainy season, when the waters are running high, the water temperature in many mountainous areas is 16° to 18°C. During the dry period, however, the temperature reaches 30°, 32°, or even 35°C near the coastal areas! (35°C = 95°F).

No cichlids, or many of any other species are normally found in the extremely cool areas; mainly cichlids, however, are found in very warm waters over 30°C (86°F)!

Besides the cichlids, there's another family that could almost as easily inhabit the Central American region—the livebearing toothed carps (Poeciliidae). These toothed carps—well known and popular aquarium fish—are schooling fish that prefer the upper levels of the water, often just under the surface, thus hardly competing with the bottom-oriented cichlids. That means that there's nothing against keeping

both kinds of fish together in an aquarium.

Cichlids may be somewhat timid. Once in a community with constantly moving poeciliids, however, they often lose their shyness in a short time.

Similarly, Central American Characidae can be used. These fish school in their native waters, often in groups of several hundred or a thousand individuals. They also prefer the upper levels of water or even right at the surface. Considering the number of their species, however, the characins are rather sparsely represented in Central America.

The other fish families that inhabit the rocky river biotopes of the Central American landbridge include open-water and schooling Agonostomidae (mountain grayling), which are not of any aquaristic interest. Livebearing Goodeidae (highland toothed carps) inhabit only a limited range in Mexico, primarily in the central Mexican highlands. Bottom dwellers that are suitable for a Central American biotope aquarium also include

Constantly moving poeciliids, like this platy (*Xiphophorus maculatus*), tend to help shy cichlids lose their inhibitions and appear in the open more often. Photo by A. Roth.

various gobies and catfish, mainly Pimelodidae (adipose-fin catfish). And those are the most important fish groups of interest to aquarists.

ones, and so there's more metabolic waste in the water.

Efficient multichamber inside filters driven by rotary or centrifugal pumps have proven themselves just as well

Stones are the most important decoration. They set the territorial limits in the rear and on the sides and provide spawning sites. A few roots and robust plants loosen up the appearance of the entire arrangement. Illustration by Weiss.

Arrangement of the aquarium

Since many Central American river cichlids reach a total adult length of one foot or more, two-hundred gallon tanks would be very suitable for them. Naturally, there are also Central American cichlids that can be kept and bred in smaller tanks.

A powerful, reliable filtration system is needed whatever the tank size. Large fish eat more food than small

as large foam-filled inside filters, which are also driven by powerful rotary pumps or by an underwater rotary pump.

Whatever filtration system you choose, it's important to thoroughly clean the aquarium water and to provide adequate oxygen.

It's best to direct the stream of water from the filter outflow so that it vigorously agitates the surface of the water.

The water temperature in the tank should be 26° to 27°C (77°F). Two or

THE WORLD'S CLEANEST AQUARIUM WATER FOR LONGER FISH AND PLANT LIFE

THIS DIAGRAM ILLUSTRATES HOW OUR ADVANCED TECHNOLOGY (POSITIVE FILTRATION) HAS TOTALLY ELIMINATED DIRTY WATER RECIRCULATION, THE MOST COMMON PROBLEM OF OVERFLOW STYLE FILTERS.

Unfiltered water enters the FILTER CASE thru the built-in STRAINER. The water is forced up into the DEBRIS CATCH CUP. (It cannot return to the tank.) The clean water goes thru the PERFORATED FILTER PIPE into the SUBMERSIBLE PUMP UNIT - and is returned to the tank completely filtered.

SUBMERSIBLE PUMP UNIT

FILTERED WATER RETURNS TO TANK

PERFORATED FILTER PIPE
FILTER CARTRIDGE
DEBRIS CATCH CUP (MODELS 400 & 280)
FILTER CASE
FILTER CASE BUILT-IN STRAINER
UNFILTERED WATER
UNFILTERED WATER

three fluorescent lamps suffice, depending upon the depth of the tank.

Stones and rocks naturally play the main role here. Several kinds of rocks can be used, such as sandstone or slate. The important thing is to avoid unnatural-looking markings or inclusions. An aquarium with a hodgepodge of stones

A powerful, reliable filter system commonly includes one of the canister type filters. Those shown here are submersible.

Outside canister filters come in a variety of sizes designed for particular tank sizes. Choose a filter that has the proper capacity for your size tank.

Facing page: (top) One of the robust plants that can be used for tank decoration is *Anubias barteri.* Photo by E. C. Taylor. (bottom) For the open middle and upper levels mollies, such as this *Poecilia latipinna*, are recommended. Photo by A. Roth.

doesn't look as natural as one with only one kind.

Arrange the stones as they are stacked in the fish's natural habitat— either horizontally or vertically. Jumbled stones look unnatural in this biotope.

Set the stones directly on the bottom pane of the tank, not on a gravel or sand layer, to prevent the fish from undermining them. Take a great deal of care not to let highly piled stones topple over; you can glue some of the larger ones together with silicon glue.

Build the "stonescape" just as you like it, but keep in mind that the cichlids use the crevices and "caves" for territorial markers, spawning substrate and hiding places.

One or two large bog pine roots with many branches soften up the stonescape, forming even more territorial borders and dugouts. There's no reason not to include robust plants, too, such as giant *Vallisneria*, *Anubias* or Java fern,

even if they're not exactly part of the genuine biotope in the wild. All of this becomes even more effective and attractive the deeper the aquarium.

Recommendations for selection of fish

Depending upon tank size, we can introduce two or three different cichlid species, always in pairs. As a rule, let a group of six to eight young fish grow up together; then, after they reach sexual maturity, they'll find their own mates.

For the open middle and upper levels, you can introduce a school of livebearers, such as swordtails and platys (*Xiphophorus*), mollies (*Poecilia*) or also *Priapella*. *Astyanax* are an attractive alternate, but one which is unfortunately much harder to find in the pet shops.

For the bottom, there are several catfishes (*Rhamdia* or *Pimelodella*).

The great majority of Central American cichlids breed out in the open. Cave-breeding species, or those that are

Priapella species are also desirable middle and upper level fishes. Shown here are *Priapella compressa* (top and middle photos by H. Mayland and F. P. Mullenholz) and *Priapella intermedia* (bottom photo by M. Meyer).

at an evolutionary level between the open- and cave-breeders, are not as common. Only several smaller species of each group can be discussed here as representative of the whole family.

Cichlids of the genus *Thorichthys*, which breed in the open, attain a length of about 6 inches at the most. The red breast or firemouth, *Thorichthys meeki*, from southern Mexico and Guatemala is a well known aquarium fish of this genus.

These very colorful cichlids prefer the shallower waters along the river banks, where they establish regular brood colonies in many spots during the dry season.

The territory of each mating pair often measures less than a meter (39.36 inches) in diameter. The fish constantly stand guard at the periphery, their gill covers spread out and their lower jaws dropped open in a threatening stance.

Once the fry swim free, they often change territories, going from one couple to another, where they're simply "adopted". You can watch this fascinating behavior if you keep

several *Thorichthys* pairs in a tank with a large bottom area.

Eight *Thorichthys* species are known. Besides *Thorichthys meeki*, pet shops also occasionally have *Thorichthys ellioti* from southern Mexico, and the golden *Thorichthys aureus* from Guatemala and Honduras.

It should be understood that *Thorichthys* species are

A popular aquarium fish is the Blind Cave Tetra *Astyanax mexicanus*, which is a good substitute for the livebearers in a cichlid tank. Photo by H.-J. Richter.

For the bottom levels catfishes, such as *Rhamdia* species, are recommended. Photo by H.-J. Richter.

somewhat more difficult to keep than are other Central American cichlids. *Thorichthys* are much more susceptible than, say, *Paratheraps* to water pollution and improper diet; as insectivorous fish, they don't tolerate any protein-rich foods such as beef heart.

Also, *Thorichthys* fry, when they first swim free, are much smaller than the fry of other species, so can't eat *Artemia* (brine shrimp)

nauplii right from the start.

Paratheraps reach 30 cm (12 inches) long; they are high-backed, almost disc-shaped cichlids, that are very colorful and love to swim about. They are omnivorous, but also feed to a large extent on plant matter, algae to be more exact. They also brood in the open, one couple usually staying together in the aquarium.

The smaller (a good 10 cm long) *Archocentrus*,

As an alternative to the common Firemouth Cichlid, there are several other *Thorichthys* species available. This is *Thorichthys* (or "*Cichlasoma*") *helleri* from Mexico. Photos by R. Stawikowski.

From top to bottom are *Thorichthys ellioti,* *"Cichlasoma" nicaraguense,* and *"Cichlasoma" sieboldi. "C". nicaraguense* tends to eat soft-leaved plants but otherwise is as peaceful as the others. Photos by R. Stawikowski.

Since 1952, *Tropical Fish Hobbyist* has been the source of accurate, up-to-the-minute, and fascinating information on every facet of the aquarium hobby. Join the more than 50,000 devoted readers world-wide who wouldn't miss a single issue.

From top to bottom are *Thorichthys helleri,* *"Cichlasoma" bartoni*, and *"Cichlasoma" pearsei*. These are all relatively peaceful cichlids although *"C". pearsei* is a plant eater. Photos by R. Stawikowski.

Subscribe right now so you don't miss a single copy!

Return To:
Tropical Fish Hobbyist, P.O. Box 427, Neptune, NJ 07753-0427

YES! Please enter my subscription to *Tropical Fish Hobbyist*. Payment for the length I've selected is enclosed. U.S. funds only.

CHECK ❏ 1 year-$30   ❏ 2 years-$55   ❏ 3 years-$75   ❏ 5 years-$120
ONE: 12 ISSUES   24 ISSUES   36 ISSUES   60 ISSUES
(Please allow 4-6 weeks for your subscription to start.) *Prices subject to change without notice*

    ❏ LIFETIME SUBSCRIPTION (max 30 Years) $495
    ❏ SAMPLE ISSUE $3.50
    ❏ GIFT SUBSCRIPTION. Please send a card announcing this gift. I
       would like the card to read: _____
    ❏ I don't want to subscribe right now, but I'd like to have one of your
       FREE catalogs listing books about pets. Please send catalog to:

SHIP TO:
Name _____
Street _____ Apt. No. _____
City _____ State _____ Zip _____
U.S. Funds Only. Canada add $11.00 per year; Foreign add $16.00 per year.
Charge my: ❏ VISA ❏ MASTER CHARGE ❏ PAYMENT ENCLOSED

_____
Card Number   Expiration Date

_____
Cardholder's Name (if different from "Ship to":)

_____
Cardholder's Address (if different from "Ship to":)
                              _____
                                    Cardholder's Signature

"*Cichlasoma*" *spilurus* is from Guatemala and Honduras. It is hardy, relatively peaceful, and readily spawned. Photo by D. Conkel.

ranging from Guatemala to Panama, are cave-brooders. Female coloration is different from that of the male; females are often much more colorful, especially on the belly. The best known representative is the Zebra- or Green-fin "*Cichlasoma*" *nigrofasciatum*, which ranges from Guatemala to Costa Rica. These fish, too, form permanent pairs, and aren't different from other Central American cichlids in their brood care, including choice of substrate.

"*Cichlasoma*" *spilurus* from Guatemala and Honduras, as well as "*Cichlasoma*" *sajica* from Costa Rica are two other

"*Cichlasoma*" *sajica* is only occasionally available in pet shops but is worthwhile purchasing when it appears. Photo by D. Conkel.

species besides the zebra cichlids that occasionally make it to pet shops.

The three species of the genus *Theraps* are particularly attractive and interesting, but unfortunately only rarely are available.

All *Theraps* are

waters.

Theraps coeruleus attains a good 5 inches in length, and, as in many other cave-brooders, the sexes are colored differently: males are grayish with many small stipples on the head and flanks; females

rheophilic, that is, they are current-loving fish that inhabit rapidly flowing rivers, as suggested by their slender body build.

Theraps coeruleus spawn in narrow holes in clay or mud river banks or in crevices among the rocky debris that covers the bottom of their native

are not stippled but are sky blue on the dorsal fins and belly, which led to their name (Latin *coeruleus* = sky blue).

During their nuptials, the female shows silvery spots on her flanks. When the young fish swim free, both parents radiate a light whitish blue, from which deep

Theraps coeruleus is a current-loving cichlid that spawns in holes in the river banks or crevices among the rocks. Photo by U. Werner & R. Stawikowski.

From top to bottom: *Thorichthys helleri.* *Paratheraps breidohri.* *"Cichlasoma" centrarchus.* Photos by Heijns (top and middle) and A. Spreinat (bottom).

"Cichlasoma" nigrofasciatum ranges from Guatemala to Costa Rica. Members of the species form permanent pairs and are cave spawners. This female is guarding her eggs in a flowerpot. Photo by A. van den Nieuwenhuizen.

black stripes stand out in full contrast.

Just the play of colors itself makes this blue cichlid a very attractive and highly interesting aquarium resident.

"*Cichlasoma*" *nigrofasciatum* parents are devoted and will attack anything, including the aquarist's hand, that threatens the brood. Photo by J. Elias.

A brooding *"C".* *nigrofasciatum* that has several of its fry in the vicinity. If danger is perceived the fry will be herded by both parents to a safe haven. Photo by H.-J. Richter.

The threat posture of the Firemouth, *Thorichthys meeki*. The branchiostegal membrane is spread out to show off the fire red color and will be enhanced as the gill covers are spread as well. Photo by H.-J. Richter.

River rapids make traveling hazardous and collecting fishes almost impossible. Yet there are desirable aquarium fishes that have become adapted to these conditions. Photo by Dr. T. Boujard in French Guiana.

Belly Sliders and Bottom Hoppers: Fish From River Rapids

The natural biotope and its residents

In places where river waters have to overcome great differences in height, particularly in the mountainous and source regions, you can often find spots where the water shoots at high speed over small waterfalls and river rapids. At times, the current in such places is so strong that it's very hard to get into it to observe and collect the fish.

If you do manage to get into the water with goggles and snorkel tube, you'll discover fish that have adapted to this dangerous habitat in a quite remarkable way.

The water in these fast-moving sections in the upper mountainous areas is usually several degrees cooler than in lower areas where the current has considerably weakened. The oxygen content, too, differs from that of other water types: the vigorous movement of the water creates a turbulence that makes the water of river rapids, or the water below waterfalls, very rich in oxygen.

Both of these factors—relatively low temperatures and high oxygen saturation—play an essential role in the life of the fish that live here. Most species that have conquered these strong currents and made them their home are poorly prepared to survive in other kinds of biotopes...and aquarists have to take this into consideration.

The clarity of waters in such biotopes varies greatly, depending upon the nature of the subsoil and rocks in the region. With old, weathered igneous rock that doesn't

People collecting fishes at the Teotonia Cataract. It is here that the now famous Tiger Catfish, *Merodontotus tigrinus*, was captured for the aquarium trade. Photos by Dr. M. R. Brittan.

Most of the fishes taken from such habitats are for the dinner table as they cannot survive such rough treatment. If they live, they need a high oxygen content in their aquarium. Photos by Dr. M. R. Brittan.

Scenes of the Rio Unini, tributary of the Rio Negro in Brazil. The upper photos show a difficult rocky area where fish collecting is difficult. The bottom photo shows a seine being dragged through a shallow shore area where rocks pose no problem. Photos by Dr. H. R. Axelrod.

freely for any length of time in the upper levels of the water. They paddle powerfully though ungainly with their usually large pectoral fins and just "hang" laboriously between bottom and surface.

Most rheophilic (current-loving) fish are built more or less slender, streamlined, and often flattened to offer as little resistance to the current as possible.

In addition, there are other anatomical characteristics that enable these fish to survive in their particular environment. In many catfishes, the mouth is transformed into a suction disc with which to anchor themselves in powerful currents. Many gobies, too, have similar suction organs, but formed from ventral fins that have grown together.

Many other fish can use their enlarged pectoral and ventral fins as locomotor organs for moving around in spots protected from the actual current. Yet other species possess conspicuously enlarged ventral fins, which serve them well as struts or supports while at rest on the bottom.

Some "current specialists" have eyes on top of their heads instead of on the sides, which is because possible predators can come from above, and also because the food for many species comes from above, too.

Aquatic plants are rarely found in such

Many suckermouth catfishes, like this *Cochliodon hondae*, are adapted for fast-moving water. Photo by Dr. H. R. Axelrod.

Three different species of *Peckoltia*. These catfishes all have the sucker mouth that is necessary for strong currents. Photos by Dr. H. R. Axelrod (top two) and G. S. Axelrod (bottom).

Three colorful species of *Peckoltia*. The barred pattern seems to be common in the genus. The flattened, streamlined body, is an adaptation to fast current dwelling. Photos (from top to bottom) by H. Schultz, G. S. Axelrod, and A. Roth.

biotopes, but there are a few exceptions. Species of a tropical West African genus, *Anubias*, grow at least partially under water, but really live amphibiously. Many aquarists are fond of these robust *Anubias* species because they are well suited to a tank decorated with a rocky motif.

Arrangement of the aquarium

Can this extreme habitat even be simulated in an aquarium? Yes, I believe so. And a tank for rheophilic fish is not particularly expensive, either. An aquarium for fish of river rapids should be shallow and not too short, of course, because we're going to simulate flowing water.

Select a tank at least 120 to 150 cm (60 inches) long, 50 cm (60 cm is better) deep and 40 or 50 cm (20 inches) high.

The most important technical part is a powerful rotary pump to generate a vigorous current. It can be used

Anubias barteri from West Africa is a relatively undemanding and robust aquatic plant. Illustration by Golte-Bechtle.

along with a filter, or merely supplementally to agitate the water.

Our water temperature is 23° or 24°C (75°F).

Since we're doing without any plants, or at most are limiting ourselves to only resistant ones like *Anubias*, we can easily light the aquarium somewhat "sleepily," which suits many fish just fine, especially when they "reside" in caves, dens, crevices or other darkened spots.

The bottom is a layer of gravel or a mixture of gravel and sand several centimeters deep. The gravel should be rather coarse—8 to 10 mm, with even larger pieces here and there. Stones

Facing page: Species of the West African genus *Anubias* (shown is *A. nana*) grow naturally only partially under water, but adapt well to aquarium conditions. Photo by Dr. D. Terver, Nancy Aquarium.

Good filtration is necessary in a tank of rapids or fast current fishes as a high oxygen content must be maintained.

In a river-rapids aquarium stones are an important construction material for creating a variety of caves for hiding places and spawning sites. The bottom is gravel. Illustration by Weiss.

are important, but only one kind, not any great hodgepodge.

We can use several larger gravel pieces to put together some semblance of a mountain stream, though sandstone, slate and other stone or rock can also be used.

Flat slate and sandstone slabs, especially, make exciting as well as functional sections of the bank, where, in a rocky biotope, many fish find hideaways, territorial boundaries and spawning substrate. A bog pine root, if desired, can "loosen up" the purely stone decor.

Recommendations for selection of fish.

Which river-rapids fish are suitable for aquarium life? Many families

contain species which have specialized in biotopes like that: characins, carp, stone loaches, gobies, catfishes and toothed carps.

From the Papua/New Guinea coastal rivers with strong currents, we get the pastel goby (*Tateurndina ocellicauda*), a sleeper goby from the subfamily Eleotrinae. This approximately 6-cm long species is particularly striking because of its attractive coloration–deep red vertical stripes across sky-blue flanks. Dorsal, anal, and caudal fins are handsomely edged in yellow. Females are all somewhat colorless.

According to observations made in the wild, pastel gobies prefer to keep out of the current by staying behind large rocks. They spawn in caves or crevices, where the male guards the eggs, which are provided with adhesive threads.

At temperatures of 21 to 23°C, the larvae hatch in about nine days and can immediately eat newly hatched *Artemia*

For ultra-clear water a diatom filter is commonly employed. This filter removes very tiny particles leaving the tank crystal clear.

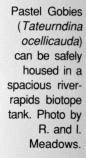

Pastel Gobies (*Tateurndina ocellicauda*) can be safely housed in a spacious river-rapids biotope tank. Photo by R. and I. Meadows.

nauplii as their first meal.

Pastel gobies, like other smaller fish, can be kept in more modestly sized aquariums. They get along well with other fish in a spacious river-rapids biotope tank. Rainbowfish, for example, with which they share their native habitat, go well with them in a community tank.

Species such as *Melanotaenia affinis*, *Melanotaenia goldiei*, *Melanotaenia maccullochi* or *Melanotaenia herbertaxelrodi* are

Complete life support filtration system, combining several functions in one unit.

The rainbowfish *Melanotaenia goldiei* comes from New Guinea rivers and does well in a river-rapids biotope system. Photo by G. Schmida.

The very similar *Melanotaenia affinis*. This is a young male. Photo by G. Schmida.

Among the more popular species of rainbowfish is *Melanotaenia herbertaxelrodi*. This is an award-winning specimen. Photo by Dr. H. Grier.

Before rainbowfishes gained their recent popularity, this species, *Melanotaenia maccullochi*, was practically the only one available to hobbyists. Photo by B. Kahl.

likewise inhabitants of the rivers of Papua/New Guinea.

A large school of these fish will keep to the open space of an aquarium, where they are a splendid sight with their bright colors.

The river rapids biotopes of the West African Zaire river have African Blockhead Cichlid *Steatocranus casuarius*, first introduced in the 1960's. Its conspicuous shape and modest needs have earned this fish a secure place in the pet shop market.

The Blockhead grows to about 10 cm, with the female a little less. These

One of the most recognizable fishes of the Zaire River is the African Blockhead Cichlid *Steatocranus casuarius*. Photo by A. Spreinat.

long provided us with a variety of fish imports, some of which have since become familiar aquarium residents. These include mainly cichlids of the genera *Steatocranus*, *Lamprologus* and *Teleogramma*.

Virtually every aquarist is familiar with the fish don't have much color to offer. Grays and browns predominate, with turquoise eyes at the most.

Adult males have an imposing air about them because of their huge humped foreheads, hence their name.

Blockhead Cichlids are well adapted to life in

river rapids. Their ventral fins have been transformed into powerful struts for support. The swim bladder has atrophied, and is no longer fully functional.

These fish are cave brooders. A male and a female form a pair and jointly occupy a cave or den where they spawn and then later care for their brood.

Other Cichlids from the Zaire River that are similarly cared for and bred include the Tadpole Cichlid (Teleogramma brichardi) or the occasional Lamprologus species.

Other Steatocranus species that have since become known include the 6-cm-long Steatocranus cf. ubanguiensis. Four to eight of these river-rapids cichlids can be kept in an aquarium of the size described here, as long as adequate hiding and spawning space is provided.

To keep these river-rapids fish company, there are "supporting" or "accessory" fish from other families that live less attached to the bottom level, and keep more to the middle levels. One of these is the Congo Tetra, Phenocogrammus interruptus, also from the Zaire River basin.

A school of ten or more adults of these magnificent turquoise green fish, the males of which sport veil-like extensions of the dorsal and caudal fins, is a pleasure to behold.

These characins–up to 8 cm long–like soft, slightly acid water.

A more robust species from the Zaire river is Distichodus affinis, a straight-lateral-line characin (or Citharinidae) measuring about 12 cm in length, which should likewise be kept as a group. This fish also prefers the open spaces, where it proves to be an agile and energetic swimmer which doesn't get in the way of the more bottom-oriented cichlids.

In tropical South America, too, there are rivers with waterfalls and rapids inhabited by

Facing page: Perhaps one of the most famous habitats in West Africa is the rapids of the Stanley Pool, Zaire. Photo by Dr. H. R. Axelrod.

cichlids that strikingly resemble the West African rheophilic species. They took over the same niche and adapted in a similar way.

The most remarkable known South American rheophilic cichlids, the *Teleocichla* species have been known only since 1988. Though they are related to the pike cichlids, they are not predatory fish, but harmless, small fish that feed with their underset mouth on vegetation and microscopic creatures. Most of these cave-brooding, largely rather colorful species don't grow larger than 6 to 7 cm.

Almost all *Teleocichla* come from a few tributaries of the Amazon in Brazil, where they inhabit clear waters near rapids; in the dry season, however, they also live in sections where the water is almost standing, with temperatures over 30°C (86°F). So they can be considered very adaptable fish that can be kept in an aquarium. Only two species, however, have been bred in captivity so far.

Various characins inhabit the same biotopes—the strong currents and rocky banks. Headstanders (Anostomidae) are found very often. *Anostomus* and *Leporinus* species belong to the larger characins, but these conspicuously colored fish are still good choices for the aquarium. They are schooling fish that

A well planted aquarium housing a small school of Congo Tetras, *Phenaco-grammus interruptus.* Photo by B. Kahl.

Teleogramma brichardi is another popular aquarium fish from the Zaire River. It is a riverine species that sometimes is called the Tadpole Cichlid. Photo by H.-J. Richter.

are best kept in communities of eight to ten individuals.

Many species prefer to keep to crevices among the rocks, while others don't hesitate to swim in open water.

One of the best known headstanders is the yellow- and black-ringed *Leporinus fasciatus,* which is found widely in the Amazon and in Guyana. It's a good 30 cm (12 inches) long.

Leporinus frederici has a speckled coloration, is also found in the Amazon and Guyana, and is also 30 cm long.

The best known species of the genus *Anostomus* is the Striped Anostomus, *Anostomus anostomus.* With their attractive dark-brown and light-beige stripes,

Leporinus fasciatus is a wide-ranging headstander from the Amazon and the Guianas. It grows to a size of 30 cm. Photo by Burkhard Kahl.

and a length of about 15 cm, (6 inches) they are one of the most popular of aquarium fish.

Species such as *Anostomus ternetzi* from the Orinoco and southeastern Amazon, as well as *Anostomus trimaculatus* (barely 6 inches long) from the Amazon are occasionally imported.

Unfortunately, many headstanders have the bad habit of plucking or pulling at the extended fins of many species, making it unwise to keep them with angelfish, *Geophagus* species or other long-finned fish. Such problems, however, don't occur when *Anostomus* is kept with cichlids that are rheophilic and live hidden away in nooks

Occasionally seen in aquarium shops is this *Anostomus trimaculatus*. Photo by H. Hansen.

and crannies.

Another group—the armored catfishes (Loricariidae)—is represented by several species in South American river-rapids biotopes; these fish will be mentioned again later in connection with other biotopes. Many Loricariidae are specialized for a life in strong currents and in rocky biotopes.

Species that remain small (up to 10 cm (4 inches) total length) include the armored catfishes which have recently been imported under the generic name *Peckoltia*, but which don't all belong to this genus.

Particularly attractive

The best known and most popular species of the genus is *Anostomus anostomus*, the Striped Anostomus. Photo by A. Spreinat.

and striking species include the orange-fringed catfish from Rio Xingu in Brazil, the deep black and finely white-striped *Hopliancistrus tricornis* (which stands out mainly because of its few but large and powerful spreadable barbed spines at the sides of the head), black-and-white-striped *Hypancistrus zebra*, the "zebra catfish," and also various striped species related to *Peckoltia pulchra* and *Peckoltia vittata*.

Several individuals of each of these small species can be kept in an aquarium. Keep in mind, however, that these fish

Anostomus frederici is also found in the Amazon and Guyana. It grows to 30 cm. Photo by Dr. H. R. Axelrod.

Several of these *Peckoltia vittata* can be kept together in an aquarium if enough hiding places are provided. Photo by A. Norman.

prefer the same hiding spots that the rheophilic cichlids do, and are, therefore, competitors!

Various Loricariidae of the genera *Parancistrus*, *Lasiancistus*, etc. grow somewhat larger. Two examples are *Parancistrus aurantiacus* from the Rio Tocantins in Brazil, and *Lasiancistrus niger* from north of the Amazon as far as Qiapoque in French Guyana.

Top and bottom: *Hypostomus* spp. Middle: *Lasiancistrus niger*. These members of the same family as the diminutive *Peckoltia* grow much larger and their accommodations must suit them. Top photo courtesy *Aqualife Magazine*, bottom photo by H. Bleher.

River Bank with Fallen Foliage

The natural biotope and its residents.

A river changes its looks between its source and its mouth. First it's a raging mountain stream, then a powerfully flowing river which can become a broad, lazily ambling waterway by the time it approaches its mouth. The landscape through which a river flows affects not only its width, depth, current and clarity, but also, to a considerable extent, its banks.

The rocky banks of a mountain stream look completely different from the broad sandy beaches or muddy flood plains of a lowland river. Such varied banks are the habitats of quite varied fish communities.

Both the number of species and of individuals are particularly abundant along banks where the speed of the river is less because of natural obstacles that slow down the current, such as small inlets, rocks and boulders, uprooted trees and their root systems, and clumps of shrubbery.

Such banks are often strewn with dead branches and fallen foliage. Underwater vegetation and relatively thick clumps of green thready algae also add to the nature of the biotope.

The open water above the bottom vegetation, debris and algae growth is home to schools of various characins—*Hyphessobrycon*, *Cheirodon*, *Hemigrammus*, and other genera with species that remain small.

The bottom, between the leaves and the algae, is home to isolated "thread" catfish (*Pimelodus*, *Rhamdia*).

On the open, sandy bottom live *Loricaria*, *Corydoras* and also occasionally small

An igarape feeding into the Rio Negro with heavy foliage and fallen branches along its banks. Photo by Dr. H. R. Axelrod.

Open water above bottom vegetation is home to schools of various tetras such as this *Hyphessobrycon callistus*. Photo by B. Kahl.

Facing page: Top: Along the banks of tropical rivers an accumulated layer of dead leaves is often found. A couple of *Crenicara* may be seen in this natural biotope. Photo by R. Stawikowski. Bottom: An aquarium for dwarf cichlids has some dead beech leaves included in its decoration. This is meant to resemble the biotope shown above. Photo by I. Koslowski.

knifefish (*Eigenmannia*, no doubt).

The most conspicuous fish in this biotope, however, are various cichlids. Large accumulations of foliage serve pike cichlids (*Crenicichla cf. saxatilis*) as territorial centers and spawning grounds. At some distance from the neighbors, each pair guards its free-swimming fry. These cichlids probably use the clumps of dead vegetation as spawning substrate.

Individual as well as small groups of young *Krobia* (cichlids related to *Aequidens*) up to "adolescent" size keep to the level just above and also in the layer of vegetable debris, just as growing "dirt eaters" or "eartheaters" (*Geophagus*), which are not as common.

The pointed-head eartheaters (genus *Satanoperca*) prefer open sandy areas, in which they seek their prey in a way that is characteristic of them—they settle down into the sand until

just their eyes protrude above it.

Another cichlid species lives right in the masses of dead vegetable matter: the dwarf Checkerboard

safe hideaways and the proper substrate.

In addition, this biotope provides the dwarf cichlids with an abundant supply of food

Another schooling tetra found in or near the bank vegetation is *Hemigrammus erythrozonus.* Photo by B. Kahl.

Cichlid, *Crenicara punctulatum,* which appears to find an ideal home here to reproduce its kind.

Almost every mass of vegetation is home to a group of two to four *Crenicara.* These accumulations of vegetable matter offer a tortuous maze of dark passages and dens where substrate breeders find

because this habitat is also the home of a multitude of tiny creatures that include insects and their larvae, to name only a few.

Arrangement of the aquarium.

The biotope described above can be created quite easily in an aquarium. The tank should be 100 x 40 cm

On the open sandy areas of the streams may be found schools of *Corydoras* such as *C. bondi*. Photo by B. Kahl.

Between the leaves and algae of the bottom are the antennae catfishes with their long barbels. This is one of the prettier species, *Pimelodus ornatus*. Photo by B. Kahl.

(50 cm (20 inches) is better); the height is not as important, but should be at least 40 cm.

Technical accessories should include an adjustable heater (150 to 250 watt, depending

Examples of loricariid catfishes. Top and middle photos are *Farlowella* spp., photos by H.-J. Richter; bottom photo is *Loricaria simillima*, photo by H. Mayland.

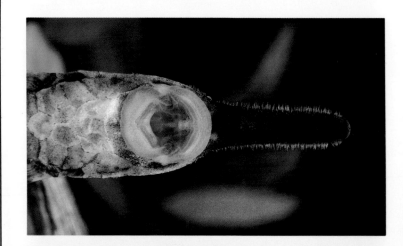

Examples of loricariid catfishes. Top photo of *Rineloricaria lanceolata* by M. Sandford; middle photo of *Farlowella* sp. by H.-J. Richter; bottom photo of *Loricaria simillima* by H. Mayland.

Crenicara punctulatum lives among the masses of dead vegetable matter. It is called the Checkerboard Cichlid because of its spotted pattern. Photo by B. Walker.

This pattern of *Crenicara punctulatum* indicates a more contented existence. The checkerboard pattern is assumed when it it is frightened. Photo by A. Spreinat.

upon the capacity of the tank), filter (motor- or air-driven inside filter, outside filter driven by rotary pump), and lighting (lid with two fluorescent 18-watt tubes).

Setting up an aquarium requires sand or fine gravel (1 to 2 mm two very suitable choices.

Lay in a bottom of sand, gravel or a mixture of both of them to a depth of 5 to 6 cm, letting it slope gently upwards toward the rear of the tank. Plant shoots of the Indian Water Star along the side panes and

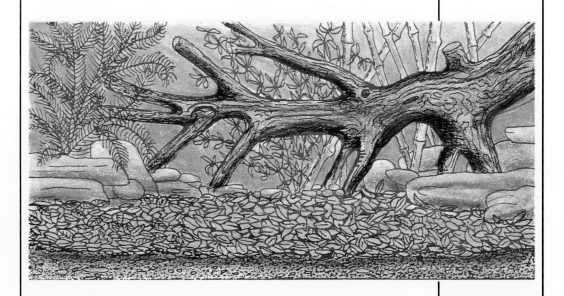

grain size), one or two swamp pine roots with many branches, and oak or beech foliage. In addition, a few aquatic plants go well, too, even if they're not exactly right for the biotope; the Indian Water Star (*Hygrophila polysperma*) and Java Moss (*Vesicularia dubyana*) are in the background. Use the Java Moss to simulate algal clumps. Both of these plant species have the advantage of being undemanding and relatively fast growing aquatic plants.

The marsh pine roots, too, are set in the peripheral and/or

The main material for decoration here is a several-centimeter-thick layer of dead oak or beech leaves covering a large portion of the bottom. Illustration by Weiss.

Small groups of young *Krobia* stay in or at a level just above the layer of vegetable debris. Shown is *K. guianensis*. Photo by R. Zukal.

background areas of the aquarium. They shouldn't be too large or massive or else they'll detract from the rest of the decor.

Oak or beech foliage (only dried autumnal foliage that's first quickly scalded before use) goes in the open central area to simulate the accumulated vegetable matter of this biotope. Pile in foliage several centimeters deep to create hideaways and hidden spawning spots.

The foliage gives off humic acids that

Small knifefishes, like *Eigenmannia virescens* live on the open, sandy bottom. Photo by H. Stolz.

Crenicichla cf. *saxatilis* and other pike cichlids use large accumulations of foliage as territorial centers and spawning grounds. Photo by U. Werner.

Geophagus sp. is one of the "eartheaters" that seek out morsels of food in the bottom material. Photo by B. Kahl.

slightly acidify neutral water.

Recommendations for selection of fish.

The dwarf cichlids are the stars of this aquarium. Whatever the species decided upon, put a group of six to ten young fish into the tank. Once these fish reach maturity, they'll start to form the territories in which they'll later spawn. You can watch your fish form breeding pairs or even larger groups (harems) of reproducing fish, depending upon species.

If you've selected the Checkerboard Cichlid, *Crenicara punctulatum*, you'll be able, with a little luck, to witness a highly interesting sex reversal. All *Crenicara punctualtum* are female at first and, usually, only one or two in a group of six to ten individuals transform themselves into males capable of reproduction.

These dwarf cichlids, even in the aquarium, prefer leaves as spawning substrate. These leaves can be dead beech or oak foliage as well as the leaves of a living plant.

Brood behavior, too, is observable in the aquarium described here. The female cares for the clutch, then the larvae that hatch (which are so well hidden that the aquarist hardly gets to see them), and finally the free-swimming fry.

Moreover, *Crenicara punctulatum* is one of the less demanding species as concerns the water quality; I've bred them even in tap water at a total hardness of 16° dH and neutral pH.

In the aquarium described here, you can also keep other dwarf cichlids such as, for example, an *Apistogramma* species. *Apistogramma* are cave or den brooders that attach their clutch underneath, not on top of, a leaf. The females alone care for the clutch, the larval young and the free-swimming fry.

Many species form harems, assuming that the aquarium has a large enough ground area. One male claims a relatively large territory, then several females move into it and establish smaller territories as spawning dens. It's a beautiful sight when one or more *Apistogramma* females put on their lemon-yellow brood-care finery, contrasting splendidly against the deep brown of the foliage debris and

One of the most popular species of dwarf cichlid is *Apistogramma cacatuoides*. This male is displaying before a female. Photo by K. Wilkerling.

Hatchetfishes are recommended to provide some activity at the surface layers. This is *Gasteropelecus sternicla*. Photo by A. Roth.

the rich green of the living vegetation, creating a visually exciting aquarium.

Other dwarf cichlids suitable for the aquarium are species of the genera *Nannocara*, *Laetacara*, *Papiliochromis* or *Taeniacara*. *Taeniacara*, however, does require somewhat more attention (the water should be as soft as possible and acidic).

The rest of the community can be small characins and armored (or mailed) catfish. A school of ten to twenty characins enlivens the middle and/or top levels of the tank. A well-stocked pet shop should have a wide selection of suitable species.

Many fishes do better when kept in schools. This is true of the Cardinal Tetra (*Paracheirodon axelrodi*). Photo by H.-J. Richter.

When keeping a school of *Carnegiella strigata* it is necessary to keep the tank covered as they are excellent jumpers. Photo by M. Gilroy.

For small-mouth charancins, there is a variety of golden, red, beige and black longitudinally striped *Nannostomus* species, which keep to the middle levels of the aquarium.

The same is true for the many, regularly sold species of the genera *Hyphessobrycon*, *Hemmigrammus*, *Moenkhausia* or *Paracheirodon*.

If you want to perk up the surface itself, put in eight to twelve keeled-belly charancins or hatchet fish (genera *Gasteropelecus* and/or *Carnegiella;* keep the aquarium well covered.

Incidentally, a school of fish consisting of only one or two species always looks more natural than a multicolored jumble of many different species. Keep it simple.

A few small catfish go

Papiliochromis ramirezi is a dwarf cichlid that does well in this type set-up. Photo by B. Kahl.

A school of *Corydoras*, in this case *C. loxozonus*, enlivens the bottom of the tank. Photo by H. Stolz.

well for the bottom. Armored catfish, *Corydoras*, are also best kept in a school of six or more individuals; they're active during the day and—depending upon species—very fond of swimming around, so that they, in the truest sense, enliven the "ground floor" of the aquarium.

Catfish, on the other hand—smaller species such as from the genus *Rineloricaria*—spend most of the time quietly in one spot. That also applies to the peculiar beaked

The middle of the tank can be filled with a school of ten to twenty characins, such as *Hemigrammus pulcher*. Photo by B. Kahl.

A school of fish containing only one or two species looks more natural than a jumble of many different species. Photo by B. Kahl.

Apistogramma agassizii is a very variable species, occurring in many different colors, making it a popular species with aquarists. The top two individuals are males, the bottom photo is of a female. Photos (top to bottom) by R. Zukal, J. Norton, and H.-J. Richter.

More variations in *Apistogramma agassizii*. In the bottom photo the pair has spawned in a "cave;" on the facing page the same species is spawning in the open. Top and middle photos by K. Knaack, bottom photo by H.-J. Richter.

One of the more colorful species of *Crenicichla* is *C. notophthalmus*, seen here at different sizes. Select tankmates with care as many *Crenicichla* are predators on smaller fishes. Photos by Dr. H. R. Axelrod.

Facing page: Among the West African species suitable for these tanks are members of the genus *Pelvicachromis*. Males of two color varieties of *P. subocellatus* are seen in the upper photos, a female in the lower photo. Photos by H.-J. Richter.

Anomalochromis thomasi is a highly recommended species for the West African biotope tank. It is small and relatively peaceful. Photo by B. Kahl.

Facing page: Top left: a spawning pair of *Corydoras paleatus*. Illustration by Sommer. Top right: *Parananochromis caudifasciatus.* Middle left: *Parananochromis longirostris.* Middle right: *nanochromis minor.* Bottom: *Nanochromis squamiceps* female. All photos by H.-J. Richter.

catfish of the genus *Farlowella.*

Most characins and catfish require the same care as the dwarf cichlids—slightly acidic water that's not too hard, and a varied diet of small food animals—fly, gnat and mosquito larvae, *Cyclops*, water fleas (*Daphnia*, etc.), *Artemia*. These can be fresh, frozen or occasionally dry in tablets or flakes.

Regular water changes of a quarter to a third of the total water volume every two weeks agrees with all of the fish species mentioned so far.

An aquarium of the kind described in this chapter can house West African species, too, especially if you're staying with the dwarf cichlids. Various species from the genera *Pelvicachromis, Nanochromis* or *Anomalochromis* go well in West African biotope tanks.

The mouthbrooding *Chromidotilapia* and *Parananochromis* species are fascinating additions for aquarists interested in fish behavior.

Characins for "supporting roles" in African biotopes include species from the genera *Neolebias* or *Alestes.*

Catfish for "bottom roles" can be selected from the genera *Chiloglanis* or *Mochokiella*, which have been imported more often in recent years.

A Lot of Wood: An Aquarium For "Antenna" or Tentacled Catfish

Top: Typical habitat in Rio Araquari (northern Brazil) for mailed catfishes that live in wood. These catfishes hide and spawn among the branches and under the bark of dead trees. Photo by R. Stawikowski. Bottom: An especially magnificent mailed catfish related to *Ancistrus* is the Tusk Catfish, *Leporacanthicus galaxias*, which was discovered only a few years ago. Photo by R. Stawikowski.

The natural biotope.

The force of the flowing water eventually erodes away the soil and lays bare the roots of the trees along the bank. This dense labyrinth of numerous small, finely branched roots offers a submerged forest haven to a great variety of fish.

Along the course of a river, the traveler keeps coming upon sections characterized by more or less thick tangles of dead wood, like trees and brush, which were carried there by the current. If you have the chance to dive or snorkel in a biotope like that, you'll find fish down there of the most diverse families.

In shallow water or near the surface of the water, schools of young characins gather, seeking protection among the finely branched roots and rootlets of the submerged deadwood.

Young toothcarp, too, just several centimeters long, hover about among the branches and roots where they find not only safe hideaways but also food like insect larvae or the tiny fry of other fish species.

Occasionally, you'll see larger cichlids down there. Adolescent pike cichlids *(Crenicichla)* have a particular preference for such environs. These lone wolves lurk in the maze of deadwood, lying in ambush for prey, and practicing how to defend a territory.

Catfish feel safe and secure among the tangle of wood and vegetable debris. You can always spot one attached by its sucker mouth to a branch or root. Its broad, flat body shows that it has no second thoughts about hanging around spots with even stronger

Suckermouth catfishes use their mouth to cling to rocks in strong currents so as not to be swept away. Algae is rasped from the rock's surface as they move across it.

Male *Ancistrus dolichopterus* have well developed head appendages and are commonly referred to as "antenna" catfishes for that reason. Photo by H.-J. Richter.

currents.

The holding power of its suction mouth is so great that, in conjunction with its streamlined body, it can safely stay in river sections where the current reaches its greatest force, such as on surfaces where the water strikes or out in the middle of the river bed...assuming it finds enough wood to which to attach itself or to hide in.

These wood- and current-loving fish are called "sucker" catfish because their mouth is modified into a real suction disk. Many of these fish eat the vegetation and algae.

Their broad bands of fine rasp-teeth scrape off green alga and microorganisms from the substrate.

"Mailed" or armored catfish are other terms for these ludicrous fish, which indeed are protected by an armor of bony plates; they don't possess any scales.

"Antenna" catfish refers to one of the best-known genera of this large family of over 600 species. The males of almost all species in this genus possess an unusual and conspicuous headdress of many long and often branched skin appendages or "tentacles" hence the name "antenna." The genus name, *Ancistrus*, is quite familiar to many aquarists.

Arrangement of the aquarium.

If you decide to start with one or two *Ancistrus* species as stars, then a 100 x 50 x 50 cm (20 inches) tank will do just right.

What we'll need for our deadwood aquarium is easily summarized: an adjustable heater for temperatures between 26° to 27°C, an efficient air or motor inside filter for some water movement, and lighting that's not too bright,

unless we're going to put some plants in, too. The needs of any aquatic plants will determine the intensity of illumination. Water characteristics aren't too important as long as extremes are avoided.

If we have South American catfish collected in the wild, then soft water (dH up to 10°) with an acid pH (under 7) is advisable. Various antenna catfish can even be bred under these conditions.

Wood is naturally the most important decorative material for this biotope. There are basically two kinds of wood. Bog or swamp oak is extremely effective, but

Corydoras paleatus is a very hardy, easily spawned armored catfish that fits well into almost any community tank. Photo by B. Kahl.

Wood is an important constituent of a tank of suckermouth catfishes. This *Ancistrus* cf *hoplogenys* seems to favor the piece of wood it is sitting on. Photo by H.-J. Richter.

rather too expensive for most aquarists to think of using. Just as useful, however, and just as right for the biotope, is the much more economical bog or swamp pine (or alderwood), which is available in any pet shop. A few very branched roots and limbs of various sizes, especially on the sides and in the back of the tank, go a long way in simulating this biotope. Aquatic plants, of course, can also be set among the maze of roots. *Vallisneria* or swordplants (*Echinodorus*) are examples of suitable plants.

In addition, some stones can loosen up the arrangement. In any case, caves and dens are needed, especially for antenna catfish, which need dark niches and crevices.

For the bottom, coarse sand, gravel or a mixture of both is suitable in a layer 5 or 6 cm thick, depending upon whether, say, armored catfish (*Corydoras*) or other fish (such as bottom characins) are also going to be kept in the tank. The bottom has a considerable effect on the wellbeing of such

Bizarrely branched swamp pine roots simulate a section of river bank where the flowing water has eroded away the soil and laid bare the root systems of the trees. Illustration by Weiss.

Corydoras melanistius is commonly available in the aquarium trade so that obtaining half a dozen or more individuals is no problem. Photo by B. Kahl.

fish...just think how the armored catfish's sensitive barbels would be cut on sharp gravel.

Recommendations for selection of fish.

Let's look at the secondary actors first, which includes many characin species, particularly ones that don't grow too large. Some of the best known species come from the genera *Hyphessobrycon*, *Hemigrammus*, *Moenkhausia* and *Paracheirodon*, to name only a few. These hover

Peckoltia are nicely patterned suckermouth catfishes that fit well into most community tanks. This is probably P. platyrhyncha. Photo by Dr. H. R. Axelrod.

about in small schools at middle levels of the aquarium.

Actual surface fish include, for example, keel-bellied or hatchet characins like the genera *Carnegiella* and *Gasteropelecus*.

If armored cats (*Corydoras*) are your choice for the bottom, then make it a whole group, never merely one couple or, worse, only one fish. In the wild, armored catfish are always found as members of larger schools. You've got to have at least six to ten of them before they exhibit their natural vivacity. The choice of species is up to you.

It's better not to include the larger cichlids here, such as *Crenicichla*, which really need their own aquarium and a different arrangement.

A suckermouth catfish in an uncharacteristic position on the gravel. It more commonly will be attached to driftwood or even the side of the tank. Photo by A. Roth.

The selection of catfishes should take into account, among other things, their ultimate size, their aggressiveness, and special tank conditions needed for their health. Top to bottom: *Parauchenoglanis macrostoma*, *Heteropneustes fossilis*, and *Phractura intermedia*. Upper two photos by B. Kahl, bottom photo by H. Mayland.

Three African catfishes that are not commonly seen in the aquarium trade. When dealing with an unfamiliar species find out its characteristics before considering it for a community tank. From top to bottom: *Liauchenoglanis maculatus*, *Chiloglanis paratus*, and *Phractura intermedia*. Photos by W. Foersch, B. Kahl, and H. Mayland, respectively.

Small tetras fit into almost any tank. A small school adds color and movement to the middle tank layers. Photo by B. Kahl.

Ancistrus species possess some very interesting characteristics that make them quite engaging and likeable. The males, which are usually larger than the females and sport a "wild" headdress, occupy and defend territories and dark dens into which they lure females that are ready to spawn.

In the wild, these spawning dens can be hollows in deadwood, clefts and openings in the maze of branches, or empty spaces between branches.

The female sticks her clutch of large, yolk-rich yellow or orange eggs to the ceiling of one of the walls of her den, where the male fertilizes it at once.

After fertilization, the male doesn't let any other fish of his species into his territory. He remains alone in the den and ventilates the clutch by steady fanning with his pectoral and ventral fins; this keeps the water circulating to bring fresh oxygen and carry away pollutants such as metabolic wastes.

It takes two weeks before the young cats can leave the protective custody of their father and get along on their own. So "antenna" catfish provide very sophisticated brood care, which is reminiscent of that of various cichlids.

Besides *Ancistrus* species, there are other armored cats that greatly resemble the antenna catfish in shape, size and lifestyle, and also do well in an aquarium like the one described here. Some of the many new fish now available are mentioned below.

In the summer of 1989 an aquarist in the

The Neon Tetra (*Paracheirodon innesi*) looks its best against a dark background. It requires very acid water and should only be kept with fishes of similar requirements. Photo by B. Kahl.

Just as in the other biotope tanks, hatchetfishes, such as *Gasteropelecus maculatus*, are recommended for the upper layers. Photo by A. Norman.

Facing page: An attractive tetra for the middle layers is *Moenkhausia pittieri*. Photo by B. Kahl.

drainage area of the Rio Tocantin in eastern Brazil discovered a 12-cm long armored catfish that resembled *Ancistrus* in body shape, finnage and design pattern, but conspicuously marked with large round orange spots at the base of the caudal, ventral and dorsal fins.

A uniformly black *Ancistrus* (?), imported from the Rio Araguaia, is extremely flat and broad (like a pancake). Males have a dense tangle of skin outgrowths on the frontal part of the head, but they're not branched like those of one of the most "attractive" antenna catfish—*Ancistrus cf. hoplogenys* or white-edged antenna catfish (first bred in captivity in 1989).

How many of these primeval armored creatures can we put together in an aquarium like the one we've described here?

Since the males are territorial, we'll limit the number to two of them, but with four to six females to keep them company. Do that only if you keep only one species in the aquarium. For two different species, then use only one male of each species; they are aggressive towards other species. Split the number of females, too, giving each male only two or three females.

With a little luck, you'll be able to observe exciting reproductive behavior without even having to set up any special conditions for breeding.

The White-edged Antenna Catfish (*Ancistrus* sp. cf. *hoplogenys*) is one of the more attractive of the antenna catfishes. Photo by B. Kahl.

Overgrown Bank

The natural biotope and its residents.

A lush vegetation is certainly part of this arrangement. In nature, however, things don't look quite as orderly as in a Dutch aquarium. There are habitats, of course, covered with a thick growth of vegetation, but not decorated harmoniously with different species of matching colors and forms as in a stage set. Quite the contrary.

Aquatic plants luxuriating around a stream, river or pond are usually of only one kind, which spreads out and takes over a lot of ground.

Biotopes with real underwater flora are not as frequently found as are waters in which swamp or marsh plants grow temporarily submerged only when high waters and flooding occur.

The situation is similar

Numerous aquarium plants are available for biotope tanks representing luxuriant bank vegetation. Photo by A. van den Nieuwenhuizen.

Few aquarium scenes are more attractive than healthy fishes in a tank that is luxuriantly planted. Photo by W. Tomey.

in biotopes characterized by thick growths of plants whose leaves spread out on the water's surface, such as many *Cryptocorne* and water lilies. Their thin stems often form a dense maze under water, while their large leaves spread out over the water's surface to diffuse the lighting.

This is also the case for many other bodies of water, especially sluggishly flowing or standing ones that are often out in open country and exposed to intense sunlight. Water Lettuce (*Pistia stratiotes*) and Water Hyacinth (*Eichhornia crassipes*), for example, cover large areas of standing water as well as the banks themselves in the tropics and subtropics.

No matter how different individual plant biotopes are in respect to species represented, water velocity, and so on, they do have many characteristics in common. They are the preferred habitat of a multitude of fish.

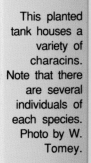

This planted tank houses a variety of characins. Note that there are several individuals of each species. Photo by W. Tomey.

Water Lettuce (*Pistia stratiotes*) are floating plants that reduce the intensity of light reaching the lower layers of standing waters.

This is the inflorescence of the Water Hyacinth (*Eichhornia crassipes*). This plant reproduces very rapidly. Photo by H. Schopfel.

A well planted tank housing a variety of different fishes from barbs to platies. Photo by W. Tomey.

Biotopes like these are found in the tropics on all continents, and numerous fish species from them appear in our tanks. Think of the many labyrinth fish of southeast Asia and Africa, the numerous characins from African and American waters, the predatory perch from Asia, Africa and America, the many dwarf cichlids, knifefish, Nile perch, catfish, and many other fish families.

It's often astonishing to discover just what dragging a net or bucket through an underwater thicket of plant growth will bring to light. Small, harmless insectivorous fish find refuge there from predators, but so do the predators who specialize in eating the smaller species. Then there are the vegetarians like the sucking catfish that rasp off algal growth and the leaves of higher plants as well.

Though most fish find concealment and protection in this kind of habitat, many species

Facing page:
Top: Standing water in a tropical rainforest that is exposed to strong sunlight often exhibit a thick plant growth; this pond is mostly overgrown with water lilies. Photo by R. Stawikowski. Bottom: Predominantly small South American tetras are kept in this aquarium, which is furnished with driftwood and plants.

spawn and brood there as well.

Many characins and barbs prefer to spawn in this finely meshed maze of plants, where their eggs are—at least to a certain extent—safe from egg predators.

Hatchlings and tiny fry, too, find an ideal habitat here in the underwater thicket, where they can find their first meals (micro-organisms) and adequate refuge from predators, thus assuring that at least some of the brood survives to grow into active members of a school of their fellow fish.

Some fish use plant leaves, stems or other parts as a substrate (or base) for attaching their eggs. Many characins, carp, catfish and cichlids attach their eggs to specific parts of a plant. Many Hemiodontidae and cichlids prefer the upper surfaces of large leaves upon which to stick their eggs. Others prefer the underside of the leaves, such as many armored catfish (*Corydoras*), the harlequin *Rasbora*,

Rasbora heteromorpha, or Nandidae. Yet other fish prefer to stick their eggs on the vertical stems of plants, such as various cichlids, armored catfish, including many mailed catfish (*Farlowella*, *Sturisoma*).

Some species even build real nests from plant parts. Many labyrinth fish construct bubblenests several centimeters thick at the water's surface, using fragments of plants and air bubbles (like froth or foam) that they coat with saliva. The bubbles stick together, providing a certain amount of solidity...and a nursery in which the eggs mature and hatch under the father's watchful eye until they are ready to make it on their own.

There are fish that build nests of plant material on the bottom, where males lure females that are ready to spawn. The European three-spined stickleback (*Gasterosteus aculeatus*) is an example.

In summary, plants play the most varied roles in the lives of many

The Harlequin Rasbora (*Rasbora heteromorpha*) prefers to deposit their eggs on the underside of leaves. Photos by H.-J. Richter.

fish. Plants provide refuge, shelter, food, spawning grounds and even construction materials.

Arrangement of the aquarium.

Pet shops offer a wide variety of aquatic plants with which to simulate a biotope characterized by further decoration.

A few general remarks may be appropriate here. The fewer plant species we have in a tank, the more natural it looks. On the other hand, the idea of a biotope aquarium should not be taken too narrowly.

The first step is to select the right plants for

overgrown vegetation. Only a few of the less demanding species are mentioned here, so we can plant them thickly in the rear and to the sides of the aquarium. These plants grow tall, thus framing the scenario with a decoration that provides shelter and hideaways for many fish, as well as a visually pleasing backdrop for simulating specific underwater scenes, that is, if we want to keep fish that need fine-leaved plants for their well-being, then we have to give them a home in which such plants grow in the thickest possible clumps. If, on the other hand, the fish we are keeping need large-leaved plants onto which to stick their eggs, then

Tall, densely growing bunch plants create a real aquatic jungle at the sides and back of the aquarium. Low-growing plants fill in the front in the middle. Illustration by Weiss.

we have to provide them.

Most fish species, we assume, are really unconcerned about whether they live in an aquarium that contains plants from their own aquarium with rocky or sandy bottom or fast-running water!

Set all the stemmed plants in groups, not individually, for a more natural look. In nature,

A well thought out planted tank leaves enough room in the front and center for viewing the fishes. Photo by B. Kahl.

native habitat, or whether they live in an aquarium containing plants from quite another continent. The important point is that we don't put fish that are native to (and comfortable in) lush vegetation, in an too, stemmed plants grow in dense groups. The fine-leaved plants include relatively easy-to-grow species such as the Brazilian Water Milfoil (*Myriophyllum aquaticum*), the Feathered or Plumed Milfoil (*Myriophyllum*

Cabomba caroliniana is a fine-leaved plant that is relatively easy to grow. It is easily satisfied as far as water conditions are concerned. Photo by R. Zukal.

scabratum) and *Cabomba caroliniana*. These three species are easily satisfied as far as water characteristics are concerned, and do well at water temperatures of 22° to 25°C (*Myriophyllum scabratum*) or even 28°C.

Of the following species of stemmed plants with small to moderately sized leaves, the following species can be recommended: *Hygrophila polysperma* (Indian Water Star), *Hygrophila stricta*, and *Hygrophila corymbosa*, which, however, has relatively large leaves.

None of the three of the above species need any great amount of light, or any special water conditions. They tolerate water temperatures from

22° to 28°C.

Another plant that's likewise suitable for use along the side panes and in the background is *Ludwigia palustris* x *repens*, which grows under the same conditions as the species mentioned immediately above.

Plant low-growing species in the foreground and middle areas of the aquarium to leave enough free swimming space. For this, use mainly plants that grow from rhizomes and that remain more or less flat.

It's not always a simple matter to combine such plants with taller and fast-growing stemmed species, because each kind can have very different lighting needs. Many low-growing flat plants that propagate by rhizomes need strong lighting. The plants mentioned here, however, are among the least demanding.

The swimming or floating sag, or dwarf arrowhead or arrow wort (*Sagittaria subulata* var. *pusilla*) is especially robust and well suited

Ludwegia natans is suitable for aquaria and has a delicate pink underside to the leaf. It should be placed at the sides or back of the tank. Photo by T. J. Horeman.

for the foreground. The same is true for the grass-like junior Amazon Swordplant (*Echinodorus tenellus*). Both species grow in slightly acidic as well as in slightly alkaline water at temperatures between 22° and 28°C (79°F).

Finally, there are a few larger rhizome plants that can perform several functions—as an independent attraction, and also as a substrate for attaching eggs. *Echinodorus parviflorus* (good for aquariums that aren't too high) is one, and *Echinodorus amazonicus* is another.

The first attains a height of about 20 cm (8 inches), and the second one about 40 cm. Both tolerate temperatures of 23° to 28°C, and both do well in moderately bright light, that is, they're not excessively light-hungry.

A moderately tall plant for the foreground and middle areas is Walker's Crypt (*Cryptocoryne walkeri*), an Araceae or arum family species from Sri Lanka (an older name for Ceylon, which is now the country's official name). This arum species is among the least demanding species of the genus, and does

Facing page: Top:*Hygrophila corymbosa*, with small to moderate sized leaves, is one of the highly recommended species. Photo by F. Möhlmann. Bottom: Other species of *Hygrophila* with the same requirements can be substituted. This is *Hygrophila difformis*. Photo by F. Möhlmann.

For a well-planted South American tank schools of tetras are recommended, such as this *Hemigrammus ocellifer*. Photo by B. Kahl.

well in slightly acidic as well as in slightly alkaline water at temperatures between 23° and 28°C.

The Water Horn Fern, *Ceratopteris cornuta*, and the Floating Horn Fern, *Ceratopteris pteridioides*, are among the less demanding species. The first of these is native to tropical Africa, and the second is widely spread throughout the tropics. Both tolerate slightly acidic to slightly alkaline water and temperatures of 20° to about 28°C.

Riccia fluitans, the Crystalwort, is thickly branched, forming thick mats on the water's surface. This widely distributed floating plant is likewise rather undemanding, and also tolerates slightly acidic as well as slightly alkaline water at temperatures from under 20° to 30°C (86°F)!

The "framing" effect produced by tall plants at the sides and back can be added to and loosened up somewhat by the use of low plants in the foreground and other items such as bog pine roots or stones. Then, depending upon

This "window" type effect was created by cutting the circle out of a wood panel placed in front of the aquarium. Photo by Dr. D. Terver, Nancy Aquarium.

the particular needs of the fish species you've selected, you can add coconut shell halves, cork oak bark or dried beech and oak foliage.

Recommendations for selection of fish

Many kinds of fish would feel comfortable in the aquarium described here. Suitable species are available from virtually all continents. Three kinds of fish communities that go well in a 100 x 50 x 50 centimeter (20 inches) aquarium are described below for South America,

West Africa and southeast Asia.

1. SOUTH AMERICA

For a South American aquarium with plants, species of the following families are suitable: characins, knifefish, dwarf cichlids, and armored (or mailed) catfish.

Particularly suitable are the smaller characin species from such genera as *Hyphessobrycon*, *Hemigrammus*, *Moenkhausia* and *Paracheirodon*, as well as the attractive, ornamental pencilfish of

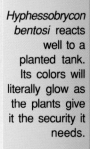

Hyphessobrycon bentosi reacts well to a planted tank. Its colors will literally glow as the plants give it the security it needs.

the genus *Nannostomus* and the top-oriented hatchet fish *Gasteropelecus* and *Carnegiella*. These fish keep to the middle and top levels in small schools of at least eight to ten fish. Though they prefer to swim in the open spaces at the front and in the central section of the tank, they do occasionally retreat into the dense vegetation.

The small bottom characins of the genus *Characidium*, wonderfully suitable for sprucing up the lower levels of the aquarium, don't hover freely out in the open, but "hop" around over the bottom.

Only the smaller species of the knifefish family (Gymnotidae) are suitable for life in modestly sized (that is, one-meter-long) aquariums.

A species often available at pet shops is the green knifefish (*Eigenmannia virescens*), which is likewise best kept in small schools; it

Along with *Hyphessobrycon* species, many *Hemigrammus* can be added to the planted tank, such as *Hemigrammus pulcher*. Photo by B. Kahl.

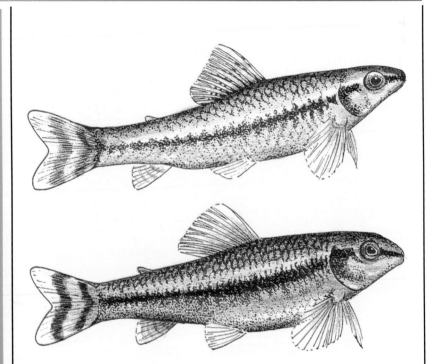

Male (top) and female (bottom) Darter Characin (*Characidium fasciatum*) from South America. The females are more rounded than the males. Illustration by Golte-Bechtle.

swims both forwards and backwards through the plant thickets.

A dwarf cichlid, from the genus *Apistogramma*, for example, lives in the lower part of the aquarium. Aquarists usually provide it with coconut shell halves, broken clay flowerpots or stone piles as spawning dens. In a densely planted aquarium, however, you can sometimes observe this fish sticking its eggs to the underside of large leaves or the underside of dead oak or beech leaves. This behavior is really closer to what they do in the wild.

The species *Crenicara maculatum* and *Crenicara filamentosum* are suitable, too. They lay their eggs on the upper surfaces of the leaves of stemmed plants, for instance, which grow more or less horizontally.

The plant thickets in our aquarium also make good homes for species of the armored catfish family, particularly the needle-like catfish of the genus *Farlowella*, which occasionally live in dense reeds or grassy tufts along river banks. They are exceedingly well camouflaged by their inconspicuous shape and motionless way of life—affixed by a suction mouth to plant stems—amid the dense vegetation.

In addition to the *Characidium* for the bottom, you can still add a few armored catfish (*Corydoras*). Though large schools of *Corydoras* are often found over open sandy bottoms, these little catfish are also seen in heavily vegetated biotopes. In this way, all parts of the aquarium are occupied without any interspecies quarreling.

In fact, this arrangement comes quite close to the actual conditions found along a densely vegetated bank of a river in South America.

2. WEST AFRICA

A West African aquarium can be similar to the South American one since characins and cichlids live there, too.

An example of West African characins that don't grow too large are the *Nannaethiops* species, which, however, are not as common in pet shops as most of the South American characins.

Among the most beautiful of African

The Green Knifefish (*Eigenmannia virescens*) is best kept in schools. It swims both forward and backward through plant thickets. Photo by Dr. H. R. Axelrod.

A school of pencilfishes, for example *Nannostomus eques*, looks better in a well-planted tank and they may even spawn in the plants. Photo by B. Kahl.

Facing page: The bright red of the Cardinal Tetra (*Paracheirodon axelrodi*) contrasts nicely with the greens of the plants. Photo by B. Kahl.

Some African tetras that should be kept in planted aquaria. From top to bottom: *Lepidarchus adonis, Nannaethiops unitaeniatus,* and *Distichodus maculatus.* Photos by W. Foersch, H.-J. Richter, and B. Kahl.

Pseudepiplatys annulatus prefers soft, acidic water. Because of its size it cannot be kept with larger fishes. Photo by H.-J. Richter.

characins, no doubt, is *Neolebias ansorgei*, which grows to three or four centimeters. African *Nannocharax* are almost confusingly similar to their new world cousins, the South American *Characidium*, in body shape, coloration and finnage.

Various pike-like fish from the egg-laying tooth carp family are quite suitable as top-level fish; the genus *Epiplatys* contains quite a few species that not only like to seek refuge under the cover of floating plants, but also lay their eggs on the fine roots. Familiar and regularly available species include *Epiplatys dageti*, *Epiplatys sexfasciatus* and the small but more demanding *Pseudepiplatys annulatus*, which, because of its dwarfism and preference for soft, acidic water, shouldn't be kept with larger, overly vivacious fish.

The smaller feather-whiskered catfish (Mochokidae), especially the genera *Leptoglanis* and *Chiloglanis*, are the

African tetras recommended for the planted aquaria. From top to bottom: *Arnoldichthys spilopterus, Nannocharax fasciatus,* and *Ladigesia roloffi*. Photos by H.-J. Richter (top and center) and B. Kahl (bottom).

African tetras recommended for the planted aquaria. From top to bottom: *Hemigrammopetersius interruptus, Arnoldichthys spilopterus,* and *Nannocharax* sp. Photos by H.-J. Richter.

African counterpart to the South American armored catfish. The suction mouth and body shape of these African catfish reveal that they live in habitats similar to those of many of the South American Loricariidae. Unfortunately, these African catfish are not regularly available in pet shops.

3. SOUTHEAST ASIA

The labryinth fish (Belontiidae) are a family of southeast Asian fish whose members exhibit interesting behavior and splendid coloration, and are favorites in the densely planted biotope aquariums of aquarists, but they are predatory.

Overgrown or heavily vegetated biotopes are the habitat of many bubblenest-building species, such as the genera *Trichogaster*, *Trichopsis* and *Colisa*.

Males establish territories directly under the surface of the water, where they construct their nests of saliva-

Facing page: Epiplatys dageti not only seek shelter in plants but also lay their eggs in the fine roots. Photo by H.-J. Richter.

Overgrown or heavily vegetated biotopes are the habitat of many bubblenest-builders such as *Trichogaster leeri*. Photo by B. Kahl.

coated air bubbles, usually with the help of bits and pieces of plants.

When the nest is finished, couples spawn right under it. The eggs rise to the surface or sink to the bottom, *Trichogaster* species, such as the Pearl or Mosaic Gourami (*Trichogaster leeri*), the Three-Spot Gourami (*Trichogaster trichopterus*) with its variety of cultivated

Trichogaster trichopterus has many different cultivated strains that an aquarist can choose from. Photo by B. Kahl.

depending upon the species.

The males, but also the females of many species, collect the eggs by mouth and spit them into the nest, where the males guard them. The young fish that hatch in a few days stay in the nest until they are capable of finding their own food.

The best known and most popular bubblenest builders are the somewhat larger

forms, and the Snake-skinned Gourami (*Trichogaster pectoralis*). All of these species attain total lengths of 10 to 20 cm (8 inches).

Colisa species, on the other hand, don't grow as large. Particularly popular and colorful species are the Honey Gourami (*Colisa chuna*), and the Dwarf Gourami, (*Colisa lalia*).

The dwarfs include the croaking dwarf gouramis

Among the smaller gouramis is *Colisa chuna*, the Honey Gourami. This pair is spawning under their bubblenest. Photo by H.-J. Richter.

Facing page: Pseudosphromenus cupanus builds its bubblenest on the underside of a leaf, well hidden from predatory eyes. Photos by H.-J. Richter.

Trichoposis pumila and *Trichopsis vittata* as well as the dwarf gouramis of the genera *Parosphromenus* and *Pseudosphromenus*.

Don't forget the Siamese Fighting Fish, *Betta splendens*, which is particularly noted for its magnificently cultivated veiled fins.

You can keep a small school of a small cyprinids, say from the genus *Rasbora*, at the lower levels of the same aquarium. The Harlequin or Red Rasbora, *Rasbora heteromorpha*, is probably the best known representative. These fish have a remarkable spawning behavior. They stick their eggs under wide plant leaves, so need plants with more or less horizontal leaves or stemmed plants with large leaves.

Other suitable *Rasbora* species include the Red-finned Rasbora, (*Rasbora borapetensis*); the Yellow rasbora (*Rasbora elegans)*, the "Beautiful-finned" Rasbora, and the Red-striped Rasbora (*Rasbora pauciperforata).*

Colisa lalia, the Dwarf Gourami, often incorporates available plants into its bubblenest. Photo by J. Elias.

The Harlequin Rasbora (*Rasbora heteromorpha*) require plants with broad horizontal leaves for spawning. Photo by B. Kahl.

Other fishes, such as the barbs, for example, also provide many schooling fish, small groups of which can go along with labyrinthine fish in a densely planted southeast Asian biotope aquarium.

The bottom of the aquarium can be left to a few loaches. These are the slim, worm-like thorn-eyes of the genus *Pangio*, but also the many, often unfortunately somewhat intolerable species of the genus *Botia*. The Clown or Tiger Loach, *Botia macracanthus*, and the Checkered Clown Loach, *Botia sidthimunki*, are probably the best known and most often kept ones, though *Botia macracanthus* attains a stately length of over 20cm.

The trunk or snout thorn-eye, *Acantopsis dialuzona*, which likes to burrow down into the sandy bottom, strikes the observer as quite unusual. You can occasionally catch a glimpse of its head peering up out of the sand.

Southeast Asia holds a store of other species from other families, too, that go well in densely planted aquariums. Unfortunately, we can't cover them all here.

Acantopsis choirorhynchos. Photo by B. Kahl.

Betta splendens. Photo by B. Kahl.

Rocky Shore or Beach Zone: Colorful Fish Among Large Stones

Facing page: Top: Underwater photograph of a typical rocky shore in Lake Malawi (Cape Maclear, Thumbi West, depth 6 meters) that is teeming with mbuna (rock dwelling cichlids) of the genera Melanochromis and Pseudotropheus. Photo by A. Spreinat. Bottom: This aquarium was set up with large lava chunks to simulate a section of the rocky shore zone of Lake Malawi and houses Pseudotropheus lombardoi. Photo by R. Stawikowski.

The natural biotope and its residents.

Cichlids from the large African lakes, Malawi and Tanganyika, are among the most popular, most frequently imported and bred freshwater fish. Their German name Buntbarsche—colorful perch—indicates their extraordinarily splendid coloration. The species from Lake Malawi are especially colorful, more so than is usual for freshwater fish. When they were first imported into Germany in the 1960's, they were called "freshwater coral fish." Dr. Axelrod brought them into the hobby and into his book in 1956!

One group of over 400 Lake Malawi cichlid species is well known to aquarists as *mbuna*, a native name applied to about ten genera with the common characteristics of strikingly conspicuous colorations and their manner of eating.

Mbuna cichlids usually feed on algal growth (including the tiny creatures in it) covering the rocks.

Mbunas are well suited to aquarium life, as you might well imagine. They don't grow too big (8 to 12 cm at most total length, though species of the genus *Petrotilapia* can attain 20 cm 8 inches), are easily cared for and bred, and their natural habitat can be simulated by rather simple means.

Mbunas live along those parts of the shore or beaches of Lake Malawi that are rocky. The underwater photographs shows how this rocky zone with its horizontal, vertical and smooth faces is quite densely populated by

Typical biotopes of Lake Tanganyika. Top to bottom: *Julidochromis marlieri* pair in nest. *Neolamprologus toae* guarding fry. *Neolamprologus falcicula* guarding spawning site. Photos by P. Brichard.

Typical biotopes of Lake Tanganyika. Top to bottom: *Julidochromis ornatus* guarding nest. A swarm of *Neolamprologus toae* fry. *Neolamprologus falcicula* in front of nest. Photos by P. Brichard.

fish. The population, of course, depends upon the food supply. The more intense the sunshine, the greater the food in the form of algae; the greater the food supply, the denser the fish population.

There are often huge schools of mbuna cichlids of the most diverse kinds that swim above, alongside or among the rocks and boulders, constantly approaching the rocks to

horizontal surface.

That's because their mouth is directly forward. Other fish can graze from horizontal surfaces while in a normal horizontal swimming position; that's because their mouth is underneath and directed downward. So it becomes clear why these fish—the *Labeotropheus* species— have to assume a different position to feed from a vertical rocky

A male *Cyathopharynx furcifer* hovering over his nest. Photo by P. Brichard.

graze on the algae.

Fish graze on algae in several ways. Many species hover at 90° to the alga-covered surface of the rock, so they're in a normal swimming position when feeding on vertical surfaces, but are standing on their heads when picking from a

face.

A few brilliantly colored individuals stand out from the huge gatherings of mbuna cichlids. They defend smaller territories from which they aggressively expel males of their own species, and occasionally also mbunas of other species.

A male *Labeotropheus fuelleborni* from Chilumba, Lake Malawi. The underslung mouth is a feeding adaptation of this aufwuchs scraper. Photo by A. Spreinat.

Females, however, are not only tolerated but even lured into their territories. The males are decked out with brilliant yellow spots on their anal fins, and these are repeatedly exhibited to the females, which are apparently greatly affected by the exhibition.

Once a mbuna male succeeds in enticing a ripe female into his territory, they spawn as they turn about each other over the rocky substrate. The female then releases her eggs and immediately scoops them up in her mouth. The male releases his milt, which the female likewise scoops up in her mouth as she makes sucking movements with her lips on the male's spread anal fin. The eggs are fertilized in her mouth.

The female broods her eggs alone. In two weeks (or even three weeks in many species), the young are ready to venture out of their mother's mouth and make their own way around; they find safe shelter and enough food in the many rocky crevices and hollow spaces in shallow water right near the bank. They grow rapidly and are sexually mature in about six months...and the life cycle is ready to begin again.

Biotopes of Lake Tanganyika. From top to bottom: A male of the northern race of *Ophthalmotilapia nasuta*. *Neolamprologus brichardi* hovering over calcite outgrowths. *Cyprichromis* sp. and a small *Malapterurus electricus* among encrusted rocks. Photos by P. Brichard.

Biotopes of Lake Tanganyika. From top to bottom: *Limnotilapia dardennii* juvenile over rocky substrate. A school of *Cyprichromis* sp. among large boulders. *Neolamprologus brichardi* over algae-covered rocks. Photos by P. Brichard.

Arrangement of the aquarium.

The "rocky bank of Lake Malawi" habitat described briefly here

precautions. The bottom pane of the tank should be as thick as possible (10 mm or more); the whole area of the bottom

Lava rocks with various species of lamprologines feeding on the aufwuchs. Photo by P. Brichard.

can be simulated quite well in an aquarium.

To house a large number of mbuna cichlids comfortably, we recommend a tank that measures at least 120 to 150 x 50 to 70 cm. A large area offers more possibilities for a decor that recreates an authentic biotope, yet don't forget that mbuna males are territorial.

The most important decorative materials are stones, which immediately brings up the question of whether large piles of stones will break the glass bottom of the aquarium. No, not if we take several

should rest on a suitable base, such as a solid wooden board, perhaps reinforced with Styropor (or other brand of foam board). This protects the tank from minor jolts.

The rocky decor is best built to extend along the rear and side walls, and can rest directly on the glass bottom. (The layer of foam board underneath the bottom serves well here to avoid breakage caused by the cutting pressure of tiny pebbles or grains of sand under the heavier rocks.) Dr. Axelrod recommends a 1" thick sheet of styrofoam above the glass but under the sand.

Use a little silicone cement to stabilize tall piles of rocks or stones. Cementing the piles together, however, has the disadvantage of permanence, that is, if you want to redecorate the aquarium or breed the mbunas. You can't catch brooding females easily from among cemented stones if you want to transfer them to a breeding tank.

Tinkerers and do-it-yourselfers have come up with various alternatives careful with forcibly shaping foam and other synthetic materials by gluing or fastening them into simulated rocks...don't let them suddenly pop apart like a jack-in-the-box.

Pet shops carry many simulated rocks and plants. Most aquarists, however, prefer to decorate with naturally occurring materials. What rocks can you use to recreate a Lake Malawi biotope in your aquarium? Sandstone slabs, piled vertically or

An aquarium simulating the rocky shore of Lake Malawi. Rocky structures dominate, providing many crevices and niches that offer safe refuge to brooding cichlid females and their young. Illustration by Weiss.

to natural rock and stone. Just make sure that the materials and colors you use are non-toxic to plants and fish (and anything else alive in your aquarium). Be horizontally along the sides and back of the tank, give a very natural look to the setting. The numerous hollow spaces and clefts provide effective territorial

This mbuna (*Pseudotropheus lombardoi*) has the reverse coloration from most Lake Malawi cichlids—the male is yellow while the female is blue. Photo by W. Ross.

borders as well as nesting and hiding spots. Brooding females and fry take refuge here from attacks by their own kind.

Many aquarists prefer perforated stone. This attractive stone is most often white and, with its many varied round holes, offers the same advantages as sandstone with its crevices. Once these stones manage to get themselves covered with a green, algal coating (they need a lot of light for this growth), they'll really look good.

A third possibility is lava chunks. Rounded chunks of reddish brown lava go well with the habitat we're simulating, and offer an important advantage—they're so light in weight that the risk of broken glass is much lower than with other, heavier stones or rock. A disadvantage of lava is its crude form and rough surface. The irregularly shaped pieces can't be matched

Sexual dimorphism is very evident in *Melanochromis auratus*. This is the dark male. Photo by H.-J. Richter.

together very well to form anything uniform, and many a fish, fleeing panic-stricken from a predator, has injured itself on the lava's roughness while seeking refuge in it.

There are no plants growing in the rocky zone of Lake Malawi. If, however, for aesthetic reasons, you'd like to look at something nicely green, then that's certainly allowed. Most mbuna cichlids are quite happy to live in a planted aquarium.

Giant *Vallisneria*, anchored between stone piles in the bottom (sand-gravel mix), is very decorative with its streaming and undulating leaves.

Java Fern (*Microsorium pteropus*) and *Anubias barteri* are two aquatic plants that are not really from their native biotope, but do have the advantage of being robust and of being capable of anchoring themselves to the rocks, where they eventually take solid hold. Also,

The female and juvenile *Melanochromis auratus* share this brighter, more golden, pattern. Photo by H.-J. Richter.

Above and below: Although these two fishes are quite similar, they belong in different genera because of their tooth structure. *Labidochromis zebroides* (above) has unicuspid teeth; *Pseudotropheus zebra* has bicuspid teeth. Photos by A. Konings.

they aren't particularly light-hungry, and they're relatively tough, so can withstand rasping cichlid mouths.

Bog pine roots can loosen up the harshness of a stony setting if it seems too monotonous for you. Deadwood, too, is found along the shores of Lake Malawi.

Any relatively large community of fish requires an efficient filter to maintain water clarity. Water temperature should be 26° to 27°C. Lake Malawi water is rather hard (over 10° dH) and alkaline.

Although Lake Malawi fish are quite adaptable, and the young born in captivity do well in most tap water, avoid putting them into either very soft or very acidic water.

Recommendations for selection of fish.

We can keep two to three mbuna species in a 150 x 60 cm aquarium. It's best to have only one male of each species, so you'll have a total of three males at most, who will soon establish territories and then

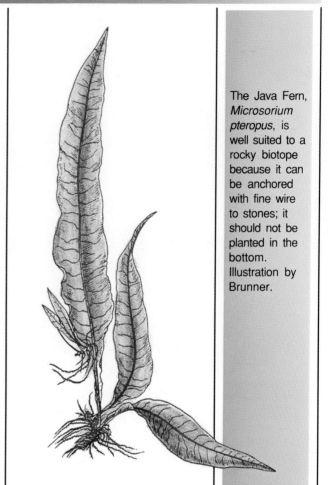

The Java Fern, *Microsorium pteropus*, is well suited to a rocky biotope because it can be anchored with fine wire to stones; it should not be planted in the bottom. Illustration by Brunner.

defend them. Keep at least two to three females with the males because these mouthbreeders are promiscuous and don't form permanent couples.

We can only mention a few representative species for all of the many suitable mbunas. One of the most familiar is certainly *Pseudotropheus zebra*, which is present as various populations in

Labeotropheus trewavasae is widely distributed in Lake Malawi and appears in many different colors much to the delight of aquarists. Photo by Dr. H. Grier.

Lake Malawi. The blue-black striped males can have dorsal fins of blue, red, yellow or other colors. Females are uniformly brown, gray or yellow and black checked.

Males of *Pseudotropheus lombardoi* are lemon-yellow when sexually mature, while the females look metallic blue with black transverse stripes.

The *Melanochromis* species—of which the turquoise gold cichlid is probably the most well known–are longitudinally striped. Males are marked with two light yellow or turquoise longitudinal stripes on a black ground color; females are richly yellow with black longitudinal stripes.

The most striking characteristic of the *Labeotropheus* species is the prominent "nose," caused by the extremely set-back placement of the mouth. Both species, *Labeotropheus fuelleborni* and *Labeotropheus trewavasae*, are widely distributed in Lake Malawi, giving rise to various local varieties.

Other species suitable for aquarists belong to

the genera *Labidochromis* (which can be called the dwarf cichlids among the mbunas), *Iodotropheus* and *Petrotilapia*. *Petrotilapia*, however, requires a larger aquarium.

Mbunas, of course, don't have to be the only fish in a Lake Malawi rocky-shore-biotope aquarium, for this habitat is home to other species, but they only rarely appear in the tanks of aquarists in some countries.

The feather whisker catfish of the genus *Synodontis* occasionally find their way to aquarists. These fish go along well with cichlids, since they've developed a reproductive strategy that involves cichlids, something that makes them very interesting to observe–they shove their eggs under brooding cichlid females...a real cuckoo bird ploy.

Similar rocky lateral

Petrotilapia generally require larger aquaria than other mbuna. This is *Petrotilapia* sp. "Orange Pelvic" from Chizumulu. Photo by A. Konings.

The juvenile *Tropheus duboisi* has a very different color pattern (white-spotting) from the adults. Photo by A. Konings.

zones also occur in Africa's second largest trough fault lake, Lake Tanganyika. Since this habitat is essentially like Lake Malawi, I'll just mention a few fish for a Tanganyika rocky shore aquarium. For cichlids, there are mainly the mouthbrooding species of the genera *Tropheus*, *Petrochromis* (extremely aggressive!) or *Simochromis*. Then there are various cave

Petrochromis sp. in general are quite aggressive, even for cichlids. This is *P. famula* (often called Blue Nyanza Lac) from Burundi. Photo by P. Brichard.

Species of *Synodontis* get along well with cichlids and some even involve cichlids in the brooding of their eggs! Photo of *Synodontis decorus* by B. Kahl.

A typical section of rocky shore of Lake Tanganyika. Photo by P. Brichard.

brooders of the *Lamprologus* group, such as the large *Lepidiolamprologus* species, for which, however, we need roomy aquariums. The chapter on the rubble or scree zone in Lake Tanganyika mentions other fish of these waters which are of aquaristic interest.

Mbuna feeding off the aufwuchs growing on rocks in Lake Malawi. Photo by H. Stolz.

There are many available caves and crevices in which the mbuna can hide along the Lake Malawi shoreline. Photo by P. Brichard.

Rubble or Scree Zone in Lake Tanganyika

Facing page:
Top:
Underwater photograph in a rocky rubble area of Lake Tanganyika (Cape Chipimbi, Zambia). The cichlid in the center is *Simochromis babaulti*, a mouthbrooder. Photo by H.-J. Herrmann.
Bottom:
Cuckoo Catfish is the common name given to this feather-whiskered catfish (*Synodontis petricola*). It deposits its eggs into the clutch of a spawning mouthbrooding cichlid to be hatched by them. Photo by R. Stawikowski.

The natural biotope and its residents.

In certain respects this habitat resembles that of the mountain rivers of the Central American landbridge: scree or rubble polished from wear, fist-sized to football-sized pieces scattered over wide areas, in some places as far as the eye can see. It begins in very shallow water only a few centimeters deep near the shore line and continues out into deep water.

High wind blows meter-high waves over the rubble on the beach, and then the water runs back into the lake, often creating a strong current.

Since the water is very clear most of the year, the sun penetrates down into it and promotes a thick growth of algae on the gravel and pebbles. The algae is home to tiny creatures like insect larvae, worms, snails, and crustaceans.

This rubble biotope is the habitat of a large number of fish that are part and parcel of aquaristics today.

The rubble-strewn shore is a typical habitat in East African Lake Tanganyika, unlike Lake Malawi, where a rocky habitat always means steep rocky faces and huge boulders on the shores.

The many crevices and niches in the rubble zone are dominated by cave-brooding cichlids. There are also mouthbrooding cichlids and fish from other families, but these are in the minority.

Broad expanses covered with more or less uniformly shaped rubble seem at first glance to be

endless fields of sand. This rubble zone, however, is no lifeless underwater desert. Careful observation reveals that the place fairly teems with fish. Let's take a look at the great variety of cichlids that have chosen this habitat.

In the shallows, just a few centimeters deep, elongated little cichlids scoot around the rocks, occupy and defend territories, court their mates, and spawn. They even defend their free-swimming youngsters.

These fish are mouthbrooders, but don't act like regular mouthbrooders (which have matriarchal families like the Lake Malawi cichlids). Instead, they enter into a pair relationship in which both parents share in caring for the offspring.

The details of the species described for the three genera *Eretmodus*, *Spathodus*, and *Tanganicodus*, vary somewhat, but their similarities predominate.

These fish even swim differently from other

Cichlid fishes in Lake Malawi congregating as they feed above the bottom on an influx of plankton. Photo by Dr. H. R. Axelrod.

Among the inhabitants of very shallow rubble areas in Lake Tanganyika are the bottom-dwelling goby cichlids. Seen here are *Eretmodus cyanostictus* (above) and *Tanganicodus irsacae* (below). Photos by Dr. W. Staeck.

cichlids. As inhabitants of the shallow water rubble zone, they are no longer capable of swimming freely at the upper water levels in deeper water. Their swim bladders are atrophied, and they move along awkwardly like the scooting and scurrying of loaches and gobies. That's why these cichlids were named "goby cichlids," and are known by that name in aquaristics.

The swimming movements of the goby cichlids are like those of

A representative of the third genus of goby cichlids, *Spathodus erythrodon*. Their swimming movements are reminiscent of the rheophilic cichlids. Photo by H.-J. Richter.

many rheophilic cichlids, which should not be any surprise when we realize that the surf along the shore of Lake Tanganyika is strong, and it would be just as senseless for a fish to hover free in the water there as it would be to do it in the strong currents of South American or West African rivers. So the clumsy way of swimming is a similar adaptation to strong currents such as in the biotope of the humpheaded cichlids in the Zaire river or of the *Teleocichla* of Brazil.

Go out just a little further and deeper in the water, where you'll find other cichlids—species that don't bounce around on the stones but prefer to move among the rocks for protection from possible predators. These cichlids, too, are mouthbrooders, but without any pair attachments.

No adult or sexually mature individuals try to hide themselves here in the rubble, only young fish and "adolescents" (or subadults) that can now get along without parental protection.

These are mainly young *Tropheus*, which brood similarly to their *Haplochromis* relatives in cm, the young have a good chance of surviving in the protective stony rubble, especially when they form large schools.

Once they grow into adults, they swim in deeper water, where, in

Lake Malawi. The females spawn with the males, then immediately take the eggs into their mouth to brood them there, without the males.

There are not many eggs, but they are as large as peas, and their yolk reserve lasts quite a while before the young use it up and are released from their mother's mouth.

At a size of about 1.5 large schools, they graze on algae. Over thirty differently colored local varieties of *Tropheus moorii* live in Lake Tanganyika.

In water two to three meters deep, you'll find slim cylindrical fish that vanish instantly among the stones at the slightest danger or even disturbance. They'll occasionally also bravely defend a den or rocky

Over 30 different color varieties of *Tropheus moorii* live in Lake Tanganyika. This one is the Blue Rainbow from Chaitika. Photo by A. Konings.

Some Lake Tanganyika lamprologines. Top to bottom: *Lepidiolamprologus kendalli. Neolamprologus buescheri. Neolamprologus fasciatus.* Photos by D. Schaller (top) and H. Mayland (center and bottom).

crevice against others of their own kind.

These cichlids are cave-breeders, most of them forming a pair relationship, and occupying a niche in the rubble, where they live and spawn.

They stick their many white, yellow, orange or even green, yolk-rich eggs on a cave wall or ceiling. Then they guard their clutch, fanning it continually with their fins to keep the water circulating. They go back and forth mouthing or "licking" the eggs as if they wanted to know if everything was alright.

The larvae hatch in three to four days. They are often carefully chewed out of their eggshells and laid in a brood hollow, where they need five to seven days to develop into swimming fry. Once these begin to swim out, their parents still tolerate them in the spawning territory and protect them from predators.

These cave-brooding cichlids include several species from the genera *Lamprologus*,

Neolamprologus, *Telmatochromis*, etc. Most species don't grow very large (up to abut 10 cm) and, besides attractive body form and finnage, are also nicely colored.

The older youngsters of forked-tail *Neolamprogus* and *Julidochromis* species participate in the care of their parents' next brood.

Julidochromis exhibits another peculiarity. It swims along, always keeping its body in close contact with a solid substrate: the belly is down when it swims over stones, turned up when it swims under stones, and turned toward the vertical face of stones when it swims vertically.

The further you go from the shore out into deeper water, the larger the fish you'll see over and among the rocky debris. Cave-brooders of the genera *Neolamprologus*, *Lamprologus*, *Altolamprologus* or *Lepidiolamprologus* rendezvous here with mouthbreeding species like *Tropheus*,

Petrochromis, Cyphotilapia or the thread-mouthbrooders *Ophthalmotilapia, Cunningtonia* and *Cyathopharynx.*

Not all cichlids live in or over the rocky rubble. You'll occasionally also see the feather-whisker catfish (Mochokidae) of the genus *Synodontis,* such as the attractive *Synodontis petricola.* This catfish is also called the cuckoo catfish because it lets gravid mouthbrooding females brood their eggs for them. Studies have shown that the much more rapidly growing catfish youngsters in the nursemaid's mouth even feed on their unwitting host's own babies! You can see this striking example of parasitism in the aquarium, too.

A killifish, too, lives in

Two species of feather-whisker catfishes that could be housed with the lake cichlids, *Synodontis petricola* and *S. acanthomias,* although the latter species might prefer less alkaline, softer water. Photos by H.-J. Richter.

this rocky-shore biotope. The Tanganyika Lampeye (*Lamprichthys tanganicanus*) is a good 12-cm long cyprinodont whose splendid coloration and graceful swimming make it quite the equal to the cichlids.

The males of this egg-laying, schooling cyprinodont shine in their magnificent, sparkling blue stippling that extends over the whole body and finnage.

They are constantly busy wooing the less striking females. Once they succeed in luring a ripe female, males press against the females next to a rocky crevice and simultaneously release eggs and milt (sperm). The sticky elastic eggs are actually slung into the crevices.

Some *Lamprichthys* eggs, no doubt, are lost to predator egg-snatchers, but a sufficiently large number develop. The hatched fry

A killifish, *Lamprichthys tanganicanus*, also resides in the Lake Tanganyika rocky-shore biotope. Photo by B. Kahl.

Cyphotilapia frontosa is a deep water cichlid that grows rather large so should be housed in a large aquarium. Photo by B. Kahl.

join in large schools and grow to sexual maturity there in the shallow rubble zone.

Arrangement of the aquarium.

Select an aquarium with as large a ground area as possible to simulate this very varied habitat at home. A good tank size is 150 x 70 x 50 cm (20 inches) (length x width x depth).

The ideal decorating material is gravel such as that found in many stream beds or available from construction suppliers and garden stores. This material's extreme heaviness, though, is a disadvantage. If you have a masonry or other similar aquarium, of course, the weight of the

Some Lake Tanganyika lamprologines. Top to bottom: *Lepidiolamprologus kendalli. Neolamprologus sp. Neolamprologus caudopunctatus.* Photos by H. Mayland.

Stones are mainly used to decorate an aquarium that simulates the rocky rubble in Lake Tanganyika. Small dens and caves are quite appropriate here. Illustration by Weiss.

gravel is no problem. Be careful, however, with all-glass tanks. Use sufficiently strong glass panes (12-mm thick bottom glass) and set the aquarium on a shock-absorbing base mat (described earlier).

Good water movement (agitation, circulation) is provided by one or two powerful rotary pumps, which may also be connected to the filter.

Don't have the lighting too dim, though, or we'll hardly be able to encourage any sizeable algal growth for the fish to feed on. If, however, we do want to foster grazing on algae, then we have to resort to other means. Gravel in a bucket of water can be left out in the garden or on a balcony in the full sunlight during the summer. Once you've grown a crop of algae on the gravel and transferred it all back into the aquarium, the fish quickly graze the gravel clean.

The water temperature of our Tanganyika aquarium should be about 26°C (78°F). Lake Tanganyika is known to have alkaline, relatively hard water. Whoever has very soft tap water and cannot or won't harden it, had best keep other kinds of fish.

To keep our decor from looking too desolate, we can arrange the background and sides with large stones, or we can plant these peripheral areas, perhaps with tall-growing *Vallisneria*, or

Cryptocoryne aponogetifolia, which cichlid aquarists like so much. Even if our fish aren't used to any plants in their own native waters, they certainly won't be unhappy about our plant decor.

Recommendations for selection of fish.

Let's start with the goby cichlids. Since they form pair attachments, it's best to include four to six individuals of one species in the aquarium. They form pairs on their own after awhile. Since the goby cichlids are just as territorial as the den-brooding species, keep only one or two pairs. All goby cichlids react poorly to improper diet,

particularly one that's low in bulk and high in protein. So we've got to avoid beef heart or *Tubifex*, and give them microscopic crustaceans, plant food, etc.

This diet is the same for other mouthbrooders, say *Tropheus*, which join in easily with goby cichlids; they are territorial, too, but not so bottom oriented.

Tropheus moorii is best kept in a group of six to ten individuals that we introduce as youngsters into the community. This group soon establishes a rank-order society into which new members can hardly penetrate. Keep that in mind when you temporarily remove brooding females and

This sandstone slab in Lake Tanganyika has an inch-thick sponge growing on it. The area is five meters deep and has a strong inflow of suspended particles. Photo by P. Brichard.

The aquarist should be aware that closely related *Tropheus moorii* populations, such as the Chimbi (top) and Chipimbi (center and bottom) varieties, are capable of interbreeding in an aquarium. Photos (top to bottom) by H.-J. Richter, H. Mayland, and A. Konings.

their offspring from their aquarium so you can raise the young separately; it will be very hard to reintegrate the female back into the original community.

Closely related *Tropheus moorii* populations are capable of interbreeding in an aquarium. That applies to the northern, the southern, or the coastal (near Zaire) forms. To keep pure lines, don't let these different forms interbreed.

The relatives of *Tropheus*, the *Petrochromis*, are somewhat more aggressive and should be kept only in really large aquariums.

In a tank of the size described here, it's simpler and makes more sense to keep, for example, a male and two to four females of *Cyphotilapia frontosa*, which are mouthbrooders and not nearly as aggressive. They are not as active, nor in as hectic a state as the constantly moving *Tropheus*, so they impart a certain tranquility to the community.

As for the cave-brooding cichlids, it's better in the long run to keep single pairs, for their pair attachment lasts quite a while, even beyond the care of their brood once it swims free.

The situation is different if you select species that establish real familial groups, such as *Neolamprologus brichardi* and related species. In that case a "family" eventually develops by itself, in which members defend their spawning den and territory in common.

Pair-forming species that grow to about 10 cm include the attractive lemon-yellow *Neolamprologus*, the likewise yellow but slenderer *Neolamprologus longior*, the attractive black-beige striped *Neolamprologus cylindricus* with its blue-edged fins, the black-light brown longitudinally striped and fork-tailed *Neolamprologus buescheri*, and the two extremely compressed (from side to side) fish

Neolamprologus brichardi establishes real family groups in which members defend their spawning territory in common. Photo by E.C. Taylor.

Altolamprologus compressiceps and *Altolamprologus calvus*, which like very narrow stone slabs when they spawn.

Large species that form pair attachments are *Neolamprologus tetracanthus*, *Neolamprologus fasciatus*, and the predatory *Lepidolamprologus* species that live out in the deeper water.

Non-cichlids that can be considered for the secondary role of "supporting fish," which were already mentioned, include *Synodontis petricola* (a group of half-grown young fish can be kept). These catfish like to swim around and

don't pester the cichlids (except for the spawning mouthbrooders). They're hardly considered competition enough to be driven from the cichlid territories.

The same situation holds true for *Lamprichthys tanganicanus*, but avoid teaming up these slim fish with predators like *Lepidiolamprologus* species, which will consider the other fish as food.

Lamprichthys tanganicanus will enhance an aquarium of smaller and peaceful cichlids since they like to keep to the open spaces. Keep a small school of them, for in the wild they live in large groups.

Lamprologus brevis is one of the shell-dwellers. Although certain shells are preferred most of these small cichlids will accept suitable substitutes. Photo by H.-J. Richter.

The relatively peaceful *Cyphotilapia frontosa* does best when one male is kept with two to four females. Photo by A. Spreinat.

Underwater Deserts: Life in the Sand

The natural biotope and its residents.

Facing page:
Top: Small shell-dwelling cichlids (like this Lamprologus ocellatus *at the door to its residence) are interesting inhabitants of the sandy bottom areas of Lake Tanganyika. Photo by R. Stawikowski. Bottom: Freshwater rays (like this Amazonian* Potamotrygon *sp.) not only require a great deal of open space, but a sandy bottom without any overly coarse or sharp-edged particles as well. Photo by R. Stawikowski.*

Wide expanses of pure sand make up the bottom of many tropical waters. Along the mighty jungle rivers of the Amazon, and in West Africa near the coast, stretch long, broad beaches extending gradually out to the deeper riverbed.

The water at those places right at the shore or bank is only a few centimeters deep, yet a multitude of fish and invertebrate species have adapted to this seemingly uninviting desert-like habitat.

The first glance usually tells the visitor that these are primarily sand inhabitants: the body is either long and slim, occasionally even whorl-like, so that they can vanish instantly down into the sandy subsoil whenever danger threatens, like eels, knifefish and loaches.

On the other hand, the bodies of some sand residents are flat or discoid so that they can lie flat and hide under their usually camouflaged backs. These flat fish, however, are also capable of disappearing underground; they undulate the body to make it vanish down into the protective sand just as fast as their slim cousins do it. Often only the eyes are left above ground to see when the coast is clear again. These eyes are high up on the head, which is still another adaptation to life in the sand. Examples of these flat fish include rays and skates, armored catfish, "frying-pan" catfish, sole, and flounder.

The great African lakes—Lake Malawi and

Lake Tanganyika—have wide expanses of sandy bottom as shallow beaches or sand flats near the shore as well as out in deeper water. Divers have made interesting observations in these biotopes and discovered fish that exhibit other strategies to survive in an environment that offers not only very limited shelter and protection, but also very few useful spawning substrates.

In both of the above lakes, it was mainly various cichlids that came up with a few "tricks" to survive in those habitats.

Mouthbrooders are less bound to a solid substrate for spawning because they protect their eggs in their mouth, where they develop and are cared for. Many other species hollow out a simple depression in the sandy bottom as a spawning territory and substrate, while still others build complicated nests.

Also, there are cichlids that erect a high cone with mouthfuls of sand that they gather and carry laboriously to the construction site. The tip of the cone contains a funnel-shaped depression into which the male lures a ripe female, and spawns with her there.

Other species build real castles, sometimes even with "towers," to delineate their territories from the neighboring ones. Complicated nests like that have been observed for various "sand" cichlids of the genus *Xenotilapia* in Lake Tanganyika. The spawning and brooding behavior of these fish occur just like that of many other mouthbrooders from both of these large African rift lakes.

Male and female turn about in a circle over the spawning substrate as they release eggs and milt. Immediately before the eggs are collected (either scooped up in both parents mouth or collected by the mother alone, depending upon species) they are fertilized. In many species, the female takes

over the task of brooding the eggs in her mouth for the next two or three weeks until they become able to fend for themselves.

This kind of brood care, however, is not seen in all sand cichlids in Lake Tanganyika. Males and females form more of a pair bond that lasts far beyond courtship and spawning. Males and females share brooding duties. Depending upon species, the partners alternate in carrying the young, or the male relieves the female after a certain time and from then on takes over further care of the young.

Various sand cichlids of Lake Tanganyika exhibit a highly interesting form of brood care—they spawn in empty snail shells. These fish are, like many related species of the rocky and rubble zone, cave-brooders that lay their eggs in a protected hideaway. These wide open areas of sand, devoid of any cover, don't provide any rocky crevices to use as dens. In many places, however, the empty shells of dead snails of the genus *Neothauma* are available, so various small cichlids related to *Lamprologus*

Sand-dwelling fishes, like this *Xenotilapia ochrogenys*, blend in very well with their background and are difficult to detect. Photo by G. S. Axelrod.

make substitute dens in them.

Many of these species—using mouth and powerful fin strokes—imbed the snail shell they've earmarked as a spawning den down in the sand until its opening sticks out at just a certain angle.

Other species reside, often as large groups, in snail "graveyards" (great accumulations of shells) where they and their progeny are guaranteed adequate hiding and spawning spots.

Still other species live in snail shells only at spawning time, and spend the rest of their time patrolling around in large schools looking for food on the sandy expanse. Males of these species are often much larger than the females, so only the female manages to fit into her snail shell at spawning time, leaving the male outside to approach the shell's opening and, positioned across it, release his milt. The water current created by the fin movements of the two spawning partners drives the sperm down to the eggs inside the snail shell.

Although the open sandy areas of Lake Tanganyika and Malawi are well stocked with cichlids, other fish live here, too. There are the "prickly" or spiny eels, for instance, whose slim, eel-like bodies enable them to slip easily down into the sand, like various South American knifefish do. These fish, however, are only rarely imported for aquarists.

Arrangement of the aquarium.

How can we set up a sand-bottom aquarium? That's quickly answered. The main item is a large, open sandy area. We need a tank with a large ground area, which is particularly important when keeping larger fish. Even with the small snail cichlids, however, a large area is good because it lets us keep several pairs together in the same tank, which leads to interesting territorial behavior. We recommend a bottom area of at least 150 (60 inches) x 70 cm, but it can be even larger, of course.

The sand shouldn't be too flat. Nest-building mouthbrooders and snail cichlids need a certain depth of sand to prepare for spawning. Also, many species that live on sandy bottoms have interesting ways of taking refuge and hiding, but they need adequate bottom thickness to do it...they simply dive into the ground and vanish from sight.

To keep the aquarium from looking monotonous, set in stones, bog pine roots or plants around the sides and rear wall. The only critical point is that the sandy area remain open, so our "sand fish" can "dig themselves up a storm" to their heart's delight.

Water temperature depends upon the origin and needs of the fish, and is usually between 25° and 27°C. Many fish from sandy areas prefer moderate agitation via a powerful pump.

An aquarium for Malawi and Tanganyika cichlids can be decorated at the sides and at the back with a few stone slabs whose stark look is offset by robust plants (*Vallisneria*, *Anubias*).

In contrast to the cichlids from Malawi and Tanganyika, which prefer harder, slightly alkaline water, South American species from sandy biotopes need soft, slightly acidic water.

Recommendations for selection of fish.

To keep the large, open sandy area from looking too desolate, we can soften up the background and sides by adding some plants or pieces of driftwood and stones. Illustration by Weiss.

A sandy zone favorite is *Cyrtocara moorii* of Lake Malawi. A good community can include two males and four to six females. Photo by B. Kahl.

Various Lake Malawi species of the former collective genus *Haplochromis* are well suited for a sandy bottom aquarium. One well known and favorite cichlid of sandy zones is the steel-blue *Cyrtocara moorii*, of which two males and four to six females make a good, one-species community, if we want only one species. This species can, however, be kept with others, say *Fossorochromis rostratus*, which has a pointed head...indicating how it feeds itself. It thrusts its head into the sand, takes a mouthful of sand, which it chews for any edible contents, such as insect larvae, worms, and so on. Whatever is indigestible is spat out or floated out through the gills. By now, you should understand why the sand should be free of sharp-edged or overly coarse particles.

Other Lake Malawi species suitable for aquarists are representatives of the genus *Lethrinops*, the males of which build

Lethrinops albus inhabits the sandy zones of Lake Malawi where it builds interesting spawning nests in the sand. Photo by A. Konings.

Fossorochromis rostratus thrusts its head into the sand and sifts through the mouthful it grabs for various edible morsels. Photo by A. Konings.

Facing page: Telmatochromis dhonti will spawn in any available cave situation, whether it is a shell or constructed of rocks. Photo by H.-J. Richter.

interesting spawning nests. The females of all these cichlids are mouthbrooders.

If we want to set up an aquarium with Lake Tanganyika cichlids, then we have two main groups from which to choose: (1) mouthbrooders—"sand cichlids" of the genera *Xenotilapia* and *Enantiopus*, and (2) cave brooders—snail cichlids of the genera *Lamprologus*, *Neolamprologus* and *Telmatochromis*. We can even mix these two types of fish in an aquarium of the size we described.

If we're keeping the snail cichlids, then add a dozen or more shells of vineyard snails. The fish will do everything else.

Depending upon species, the fish excavate their homesteads, throw up real sandy ramparts around their property, or pull and push until they've set their snail shells at just the right angle and depth in the sand.

Let us consider *Lamprologus ocellatus*, which forms a pair attachment and lives quite closely bound to its snail shells. These fish are territorial, and vigorously defend their territory. In the

Neolamprologus meeli shows interest in snail shells only at spawning time. Photo by H.-J. Richter.

In *Lamprologus callipterus* the male is twice (or more) the size of the female. The females reside in shells that are too large for the males to enter. Photo by Dr. H. R. Axelrod.

aquarium, these dwarfs (6 cm long at most, and females are even smaller) even seize the aquarist's hand!

Neolamprologus meeli, on the other hand, is polygamous (one male spawns with several females). This species shows interest in snail shells only during spawning time, and imbeds them down into the sand during the courtship ritual.

Another interesting species is *Lamprologus callipterus*, of which the male is twice as large as the female, that is, up to 15 cm. This, too, is a polygamous species.

The males gather snail shells together in a pit or depression, where the females then stay. The males are too large to enter, so have to fertilize the eggs from the outside. When danger threatens, the males flee out into open water while the females hide in the shells.

Of the genus *Telmatochromis*, we'll mention only *Telmatochromis dhonti*, which attains a length of about 7 cm. These cichlids don't seem to be bound to snail shells as their spawning substrate, for they've also been seen to spawn between stones in caves.

In the case of *Telmatochromis dhonti*, males and females form a pair bond. Both partners occupy a snail shell together, which they imbed down into the

sand and defend as a common territory.

As for mouthbrooders, we'll briefly mention only one *Xenotilapia* and one *Enantiopus* species. *Xenotilapia flavipinnis* is one of the smallest sand cichlids (8 cm long). The female gathers up the 20 to 30 eggs in her mouth, where she broods them for nine or more days. Then she transfers the young (still attached to their yolk sacs) to the male.

Once the young are free-swimming (a few days later), the mother once again participates in caring for them. When extreme danger threatens, the male gathers up the young fish, and the female defends the territory. Once the young become too large for all to fit together in their father's mouth, both parents take a mouthful. You can keep just one pair of *Xenotilapia* in an aquarium, but a whole group or school more closely approaches their natural state in the wild.

Enantiopus melanogenys grows to barely 15 cm in length, but can also be kept in a group. The males hollow out a large, flat depression with a shallow crater in the middle, in which fish spawn in typical mouthbrooder fashion.

The eggs are fertilized even before the female gets them into her

Xenotilapia flavipinnis is one of the smallest of the sand dwelling cichlids. It sits on the bottom propped up by its pelvic fins. Photo by P. Brichard.

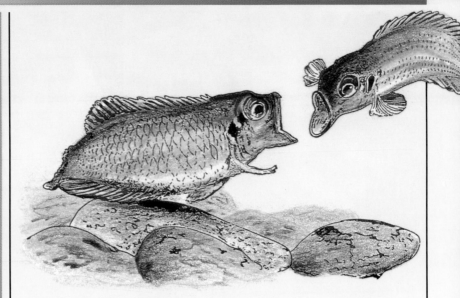

Two *Lamprologus ocellatus* males with mouths agape, defending their territories. Drawing by Sommer.

mouth. In just about three weeks she releases the young fish. In this species, the female alone cares for the progeny.

Just as many other sand cichlids, *Enantiopus melanogenys* is quite timid, like, for example, when the aquarium light is suddenly turned off. A dimmer is the remedy in this case. Also, avoid abrupt movements next to the aquarium. Sudden fright makes sand cichlids flee in panic. In an aquarium, no matter how large, a wave of panic can drive your fish into the panes and injure their heads or mouths.

South American sand

The female *Xenotilapia flavipinnis* incubates about 20 to 30 eggs in her mouth for nine or more days. Photo by H.-J. Richter.

The newly hatched young of *Xenotilapia flavipinnis* is transferred to the male until they are free swimming. Then the female takes over again. Photo by H.-J. Richter.

fish include the freshwater rays of the genera *Potamotrygon* and *Disceus*, which can attain a diameter of over half a meter; young specimens are often sold in pet shops. They are usually specimens collected in the wild and imported from South America.

These livebearers have been bred in captivity (the male can be recognized by the copulatory organ formed by its pelvic fins), but only seldomly appear in aquarists' tanks.

Three or four rays can be kept in a tank of the size described here.

Take care while working in freshwater ray tanks. These fish possess an erectable spine on the tail for defensive use. If they feel threatened, they lash out with their tail toward the supposed enemy, causing painful "stings" in human victims.

Potamotrygon motoro from Brazil is a particularly beautiful and strikingly marked species that sports large, round eyespots on the dorsal side.

The large family of armored catfish includes many species that prefer sandy bottoms. Most of the Loricariidae (subfamily Loricariinae) prefer sandy ground. Snorkelers in the shallow waters along the banks of South American rivers keep finding armored

More than one ray can be kept in a tank of suitable size. Seen here are two *Potamotrygon hystrix*. Photo by H. Stolz.

Potamotrygon motoro is one of the more attractive species of freshwater ray. It is imported from Brazil. Photo by Dr. H. R. Axelrod.

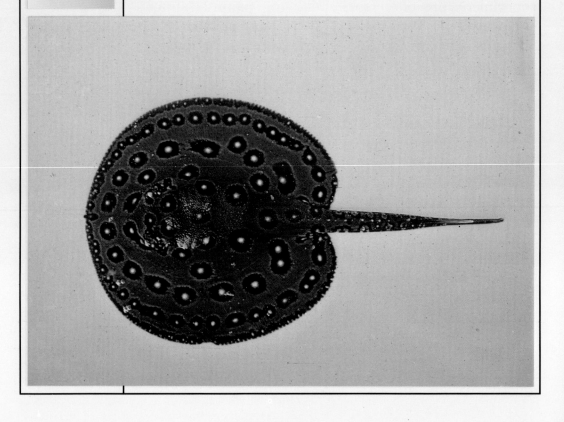

One of the less common rays seen in the aquarium trade is *Disceus thayeri*. Photo by G. Dingerkus.

catfish of the genera *Loricaria, Rineloricaria, Cteniloricaria, Loricariichthys* or *Lamontichthys*, to name only a few. With their different kinds (depending upon genus) of flat body forms and camouflage patterns of brown and beige, they are magnificently adapted to protect themselves in this habitat. Many species can also burrow down into the sand.

Another South American catfish family, the Aspredinidae, likewise includes flat species that prefer sandy areas and that can dig in. They swim in an interesting manner: frying-pan cats move forward by the recoil principle by squirting

Examples of loricariid catfishes. Top to bottom: *Loricaria* sp. *Pseudohemiodon laticeps*. *Pseudohemiodon* sp. cf. *amazonas*. Top photo courtesy *Aqualife*, Japan; center photo by D. Allison; bottom photo by Roman.

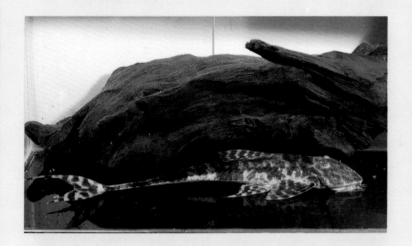

Examples of loricariid catfishes. Top to bottom: *Loricaria* sp. *Loricaria simillima*. *Cteniloricaria* sp. cf. *maculata*. Top and middle photos by D. Allison, bottom photo by H. Bleher.

Examples of loricariid catfishes. Top to bottom: *Rineloricaria lanceolata*. *Rineloricaria* sp. *Rineloricaria* sp. Photos by H.-J. Richter, H. Mayland, and H. Linke, respectively.

Examples of loricariid catfishes. Top to bottom: *Rineloricaria lanceolata. Rineloricaria* sp. *Rineloricaria lanceolata.* Photos by H.-J. Richter, H. Linke, H.-J. Richter, respectively.

Hemiodontichthys acipenserinus is a loricariid catfish from Mato Grosso, Brazil. Photo by H. Bleher.

water so forcefully from their gill openings that they jet forward!

Since the rays as well as the catfish are bottom dwellers, they can join a community in which others stay at higher levels. Schooling fish such as characins, for example, even include some members that live exclusively at the top, like the hatchetfish of the genera *Carnegiella* and *Gasteropelecus*. That adds life upstairs without detracting from the aquarium's overall character as a sand biotope.

Top fishes, such as these *Carnegiella strigata* and *Gasteropelecus sternicla*, add movement to the upper layers without detracting from the sandy character of the tank. Photo by H.-J. Richter.

Carnegiella marthae also livens up the top layers but is not as commonly available as the others. Photos by Dr. H. R. Axelrod.

Index